Dear Dani

Happy Baking!

Fondly,

Patti & Tom

ONE SWEET COOKIE

For David, who ate all the cookies.

ONE SWEET COOKIE

CELEBRATED CHEFS SHARE FAVORITE RECIPES

TRACEY ZABAR

PHOTOGRAPHY BY ELLEN SILVERMAN

RIZZOLI
NEW YORK

New York · Paris · London · Milan

CONTENTS

Introduction 6

Notes on Baking Cookies 10

CHAPTER *No 1*

BROWNIES, BARS, AND CAKEY COOKIES 15

CHAPTER *No 2*

NUTS, CHIPS, AND OATMEAL COOKIES 51

CHAPTER *No 3*

PASTRY, PETITS FOURS, AND CHOCOLATE COOKIES 91

CHAPTER *No 4*

MERINGUES, *MACARONS*, AND MACAROONS 113

CHAPTER *No 5*

BISCOTTI, SPICE COOKIES, AND SEED COOKIES 127

CHAPTER *No 6*

SUGAR COOKIES, SHORTBREAD, AND DOUGHNUTS 155

Tracey's Bookshelf 184

Acknowledgments 186

Sources 187

Conversion Charts 187

Index 188

Credits 192

I am passionate about desserts, especially cookies. One time, at an elegant New York City restaurant, I shared a cookie plate with friends. When we left the restaurant, the city was blanketed with snow. No cabs in sight. As we trudged through the blizzard and headed toward the subway, I spent every moment of that treacherous walk dreaming of those cookies. (I even imagined myself the next morning in a snowdrift, covered in crumbs, with a huge smile on my frozen face.) Apparently, I have a serious cookie obsession.

One way to satisfy my obsession would be to host an old-fashioned cookie swap at my house. Such cookie exchanges have been held in my Massachusetts hometown for more than fifty years, and in fact, all over the country. Today, as in the past, these parties are an opportunity for friends to share their favorite cookies and recipes. My happy guests would sample heaps of fanciful confections from platters overflowing with charming one-bite meringues and *macarons*, enchanting linzers and *tuiles*.

When I suggested to my friends the idea of replacing our annual museum day with a cookie swap, it was soundly rejected. These svelte women offered excuses, ranging from the necessity of a perpetual diet to the permanent closing of the kitchen after the last child headed off to college. Anyway, the unfortunate reality was that my mostly career-women friends, with their busy schedules, would likely arrive bearing Tupperware containers of chocolate chip disasters, diet delights that the dog wouldn't eat, and anything the bakery had left over at closing. Oh, dear.

Recounting my woeful tale to a friend while having lunch at her restaurant, I was overheard by one of the staff who surprised me with a plate of cookies. Because I had just polished off a delicious dessert (that was so good I had to control myself not to lick the plate), I was ashamed that my first instinct was to jam all those cookies into my mouth at the same time. My next brilliant idea was to surreptitiously sweep the contents off the plate into my handbag. Instead, I

acted like a lady, nibbling on as many as I could without looking like the glutton I surely am. The two cookies that stood out were a little orange round with fragrant icing and a mystery green one. Was it almond or pistachio? One bite proved it to be the latter.

I decided that it was time to figure out whether I had a serious cookie addiction or just a great appreciation for them. Thinking about the never-to-be cookie exchange, I realized, instead, that I could create the ultimate cookie swap with my chef friends. However, I didn't feel comfortable asking these busy professionals to bake dozens of cookies and then to share their secret recipes. It would be like inviting my doctor to come over for lunch and oh, by the way, could you do some surgery between the appetizers and the main course?

Then, the concept of writing a virtual cookie-swap book occurred to me. I envisioned featuring only New York City restaurant chefs and their creations, but eventually expanded the circle to include bakery friends and a few out-of-towners. Soon, my longtime editor gave me the green light for such a baking book.

Over the next few months, I gathered a wonderful collection of recipes. Some of the participants contributed multiple recipes from their repertoires. A number of the chefs didn't bake, but they generously provided introductions to their pastry chefs. Following interviews in taxicabs, on the phone, and at the beach, recipes appeared in my e-mail and mailbox. One recipe was scribbled on a napkin that was tucked into a box of (you guessed it) cookies. Some recipes arrived in perfect, ready-to-publish form. Others were short lists of ingredients and nothing else—150g *beurre*, 120g *sucre*, 1 *oeuf* et 250g *farine*—exactly what you might see written on the tile wall in an upscale restaurant kitchen. I began to translate these cryptic codes into coherent recipes, suitable for the home baker.

As my collection grew, I saw that it contained a delightful variety of sweets from all over the world. A few on the petit four plate teetered on the edge of being cakes and candy. A number were actually doughnuts and brownies. Some might argue that certain pastries are not technically cookies, but today many consider them to be part of the cookie family. It is my opinion that the definition of a traditional cookie—a sweet, flat tea cake, either soft or crisp, often showered with sugar—has stretched to include all sorts of treats and confections.

Over the years I have taken baking classes with talented teachers who demonstrated eight or nine cookies at a time. They were like watching carefully choreographed ballets. Some master bakers told hilarious stories about the cookies, while producing them effortlessly.

For this baking book, I tested each recipe, making two or three batches of cookies a day for months. To ensure that my family did not gain hundreds of pounds, I gave away thousands of cookies. My hair smelled of baked goods. Children and dogs followed me home.

Several chefs offered to bake small batches of cookies for the book's photography shoot. When I shamelessly mentioned that the shoot began on my birthday (October 18th), to my delight, many chefs showed up in person. Some even arranged the cookies and styled the shots. One chef made an entire family of gingerbread cookies for my children, who follow our family's rule—you must bite off the legs of gingerbread men and women first or they might run away.

During the creation of the book, some of the bakers relocated or opened new restaurants; a few left New York, moving to Hong Kong, Las Vegas, or elsewhere. Others became television celebrity chefs. I forgive them for deserting me (pun intended), and I've included them in *One Sweet Cookie*.

These recipes are for all seasons and tastes. Featured are the signature cookies of world-class restaurants as well as personal and family treasures. Whether served on a pretty silver tray or an elegant porcelain plate, or tucked into a lunch box, all are the perfect ending to a delightful meal. Your cookie jar will magically empty when you fill it with a batch of any one of these delectable concoctions.

NOTES ON BAKING COOKIES

The vast majority of these recipes are quick and easy to prepare. Although I converted a number of them from metric (more precise but less familiar to most home bakers) to standard American measurements, the proportions of the ingredients have remained the same. The recipes from restaurants have been reduced to small batches more easily managed by the home baker. I tried to retain each chef's voice as much as possible. You can learn a lot from these rock stars of the food world—the variations in their directions are like mini baking classes that provide peeks into their individual technical styles. The recipe yields are approximate. Your technique for measuring cookies may create more or less than what is specified. For example, when you use a level tablespoon to drop the cookies onto the prepared pans, there will be more, slightly smaller cookies than if a rounded tablespoonful is used.

The Kitchen: Essential Equipment and Tools

By starting with a clean, organized kitchen, you can probably do the dishes and put your pantry back in order before the timer dings and you pull the first batch of cookies out of the oven.

Stock your kitchen with the very best appliances and tools. Although you can mix your batter by hand, a KitchenAid stand mixer is a great investment. My lavender one is the workhorse (besides me) of my baking kitchen. You need only one, but invest in multiple work bowls, beaters, and whisks if you plan to do a lot of baking. The same goes for measuring cups, spoons, cooling racks, and silicone spatulas. For easy cookie forming, get three ice-cream scoops with spring-loaded handles—teaspoon, tablespoon, and cupcake size. You will also need a great rolling pin and some sturdy cookie cutters. Place a pile of half-sheet pans, about 13 by 18 inches (avoid the nonstick pans as their dark color will promote burned cookie bottoms), within reach, and invest in a mountain of parchment paper sheets. Piping bags (if you choose the reusable ones, rinse in

very hot water; never use detergent) and a variety of large tips are also handy, as are a bench scraper and a digital thermometer. You can weigh out baking chocolate and chips (which come in 12-ounce bags) on a digital scale. If your trash is many steps away, set out a large bowl or an empty, rinsed milk carton to act as your "pig." You have to dump it only once, after you finish baking.

The Well-Stocked Pantry: The Ingredients

Stock your pantry with basic baking staples. These items include flour, sugar, vanilla, chocolate, baking powder, and baking soda. Others are easily obtainable when needed. For example, unsweetened shredded coconut can be purchased in most health food stores. My favorite sources for a few hard-to-find items are listed on page 187.

Always have all-purpose flour on hand. Be aware that some recipes direct you to use another type of flour, such as cake, pastry, or whole wheat; or one of the heirloom flours (red fife, graham, and corn). Although granulated sugar is most often called for, sometimes you will need to use confectioners', sanding, turbinado, pearl, or brown sugars.

Make sure your supply of baking essentials such as jams, spices, and dried fruit (cherries, raisins, and berries) is also fresh. Nuts in particular can get rancid. Pure extracts (never artificial ones), such as vanilla, almond, and orange, are important ingredients.

Choose the best-quality chocolate available. I always keep a 3-kilogram bag of Valrhona 70 percent dark-chocolate *pistoles*, or coins, and a variety of other chocolates in my freezer. These small coins melt beautifully in a double boiler. Because they come in such large quantities, another idea for them is to make sugar cookies that are approximately the same size as the coins. The moment the cookies come out of the oven, flip over each cookie and press one coin onto the bottom. The chocolate will partially melt and "glue" onto it. You will have instant "schoolboy" cookies.

Some recipes call for tempering the chocolate, a complicated process where chocolate *couverture* is heated, cooled, and agitated to make it shiny and hard, so it will snap when broken. Instead, you can substitute bittersweet or semisweet chocolate that has been melted over a double boiler.

Make your own chocolate chips or chunks by chopping the *pistoles* by hand or in a food processor. This beats the old-fashioned method of hacking and sawing away at a big block of chocolate. If you prefer to use traditional chocolate chips, rather than making your own, choose a high-quality brand of chips. Do not substitute chocolate chips when a recipe calls for melting baking chocolate because the chips have substances added to them that keep them from melting completely.

Please use fresh, organic ingredients when possible; most everything else should be unprocessed and chemical free. Shop at farmers' markets the day of or the day before baking. Purchase seasonal fruits. Dairy products, such as cream and yogurt, are certainly best right from the source. Unsalted butter is preferable for most cookie recipes. Let the butter soften for a creamy batter instead of letting it get too soft and warm, as this will produce a greasy batter.

Although I am a bit of a snob about fresh ingredients, I occasionally make junk food exceptions for crazy add-ins, such as cereal, candy, marshmallows, and potato chips smushed into the batter. I call these kitchen-sink cookies. Try to skip the soda pop, olive oil, grapefruit, and gummy anything, which in my opinion, have no business in hand-baked desserts.

Recipe Instructions

Before you bake, study the recipe. Sometimes the instructions require the dough to rest in the refrigerator for several hours or overnight. Take this information into consideration if you want to whip up a batch of cookies quickly.

- Follow instructions carefully.
- Preheat the oven and butter or line your pan with parchment paper, if called for.

A Few Basic Techniques

A practice I highly recommend is to prepare your baking setup by putting everything in place (this is known as *mise en place*) by measuring out each ingredient and laying out each piece of equipment needed. You will be able to tell right away if there is enough (or none) of a particular ingredient, or if it isn't fresh. Go to the store to fill in missing items before beginning. The beauty of preparing your *mise en place* is that if you are interrupted during baking, you'll be able to continue without missing a beat. Upon returning to the kitchen from answering the door or phone (or anything else that calls you away), you'll know where you left off. Otherwise, you run the risk of adding twice as much of an ingredient, such as sugar—which most kids would say is a forgivable sin—or, heaven forbid, not adding any sugar at all.

Make sure to sift flour (always spooned into a measuring cup, never scooped unless the recipe directs otherwise) and other dry ingredients onto a sheet of waxed or parchment paper, and set aside until needed.

Large eggs are ideal—again, as fresh as possible. Crack each egg individually into a small, white ceramic bowl, and take a moment to examine the contents for bits of shell, which you will need to fish out. Discard an egg if there are blood spots, and start again with a clean bowl. Add one egg at a time to the batter, and then crack and check the next one. Stay safe—no tasting the batter, as consuming raw eggs can be unhealthy.

After you have mastered the basics of baking, you can experiment. Try substituting the seeds scraped from a vanilla bean for pure vanilla extract, or a whole envelope of Italian leavening (available in Italian grocery stores) for a teaspoon of baking soda or powder.

Enjoy baking like a skilled professional, and then share your new favorite confections with friends and family.

CHAPTER

№ *1*

BROWNIES, BARS,

AND

CAKEY COOKIES

MILK CHOCOLATE BROWNIES

Nick Malgieri of the Institute of Culinary Education

Master baker Malgieri has been my teacher for several years. He keeps me laughing with stories of his great-aunts Philomena, Elvira, and Nicoletta, and the trouble they were always getting into. This recipe for delicate, lightly caramelized brownies is a variation on one he learned in culinary school almost forty years ago. When he tried to scale down the recipe to make a smaller batch, he added only half the required flour. Here is the result of that lucky accident.

• MAKES ABOUT 24 BROWNIES

8 ounces (2 sticks) unsalted butter

5 ounces milk chocolate, cut into ¼-inch pieces

4 ounces unsweetened chocolate, cut into ½-inch pieces

4 large eggs

¼ teaspoon salt

¾ cup granulated sugar

1 cup packed light brown sugar

2 teaspoons pure vanilla extract

1 cup all-purpose flour (spoon flour into dry-measure cup and level off)

Set a rack in the middle of the oven, and preheat to 350°F. Line a 13 by 9 by 2-inch baking pan with a piece of buttered parchment or aluminum foil.

Fill a medium saucepan with water, bring to a boil, and turn off the heat. Combine the butter, milk chocolate, and unsweetened chocolate in a heatproof bowl, and set over the pan of water. Stir occasionally until the mixture is melted and smooth.

Whisk the eggs together in a large bowl, and then whisk in the salt, granulated sugar, brown sugar, and vanilla. Stir in the chocolate mixture, then sift over and gently fold in the flour.

Pour the batter into the prepared pan and spread evenly. Bake for about 40 minutes, until the top has formed a shiny crust and the batter is moderately firm. Cool in the pan on a wire rack. Wrap the pan in plastic wrap, and keep at room temperature or refrigerated until the next day to make cutting easier.

To cut the brownies, remove the plastic wrap, unmold onto a cutting board, remove the parchment or foil, and cover with another cutting board. Turn right side up and trim away the edges. Cut the brownies into 2-inch squares.

PECAN MILK CHOCOLATE BROWNIES
Add 2 cups (about ½ pound) pecan pieces to the batter before baking.

PALM BEACH BROWNIES WITH CHOCOLATE-COVERED MINTS

Maida Heatter

I received a copy of one of legendary baking author Maida Heatter's classic books more than thirty years ago at my bridal shower and have been a devotee ever since. There are two versions of this recipe. Her original, which does not include the chocolate-covered mints, was the one I made for my brand-new husband to keep him happy during college exams. Choose either version, with or without the mints. Following her recipe step-by-step is like taking a master class in baking.

• MAKES ABOUT 32 JUMBO BROWNIES — *actually, 6½ pounds of brownies*

8 ounces unsweetened chocolate

8 ounces (2 sticks) unsalted butter

8 ounces (2 generous cups) walnuts

5 large eggs

2 teaspoons pure vanilla extract

½ teaspoon pure almond extract

¼ teaspoon salt

1 tablespoon plus 1 teaspoon instant espresso powder (I use Medaglia d'Oro from an Italian grocery store)

3¾ cups granulated sugar

1⅔ cups sifted unbleached flour

Two 14- or 15.4-ounce bags York chocolate-covered peppermint patties, unwrapped

Adjust an oven rack one third up from the bottom and preheat the oven to 425°F. Line a 9 by 13 by 2-inch pan as follows: Invert the pan and center a 17-inch length of aluminum foil, shiny side down, over the pan. With your hands, press down on the sides and corners of the foil to shape it to the pan. Remove the foil. Turn the pan right side up. Place the foil in the pan and very carefully press it into place. Now, to butter the foil, place a piece of butter (additional to that in ingredients) in the pan, and put the pan in the oven. When the butter is melted, use a pastry brush or a piece of crumpled plastic wrap to spread the butter all over the foil. Set the prepared pan aside.

Place the chocolate and the butter in the top of a large double boiler over hot water on moderate heat, or in a 4- to 6-cup heavy saucepan over low heat.

Stir occasionally, until the chocolate and butter are melted. Stir to mix. Remove from the heat and set aside.

Break the walnuts into large pieces; set aside.

In the large bowl of an electric mixer, fitted with the paddle attachment, beat the eggs with the vanilla and almond extracts, salt, espresso, and sugar at high speed for 10 minutes. On low speed add the chocolate mixture (which may still be warm) and beat only until mixed. Then add the flour and again beat on low speed only until mixed. Remove the bowl from the mixer.

Stir in the nuts.

Spoon half the mixture (about 3½ cups) into the prepared pan and smooth the top.

Place a layer of the mints, touching each other, all over the chocolate layer. Do not cut the mints in order to put them in places where there isn't room for whole mints. If you do cut them, they will run and they will burn. It is better to leave the spaces empty if there is not room for whole mints.

Spoon the remaining chocolate mixture all over the pan and smooth the top.

Bake for 35 minutes, reversing the pan front to back once during baking to ensure even baking. At the end of 35 minutes the cake will have a firm crust on top, but if you insert a toothpick in the middle it will come out wet and covered with chocolate. Nevertheless, it is done. Do not bake any longer.

Remove the pan from the oven; let stand until cool. Cover the pan with a half-sheet pan and invert the pan and the sheet. Remove the pan and foil lining.

Cover the cake with a length of waxed paper and another half-sheet pan and invert again, leaving the cake right side up.

Now the cake must be refrigerated for a few hours or overnight before it is cut into bars.

When you are ready to cut the cake, use a long, heavy knife with a sharp blade, either serrated or straight—try both. Cut the cake into quarters. Cut each quarter in half, cutting through the long sides. Finally, cut each piece into 4 bars, cutting through the long sides. (I think these are better in narrow bar shapes than in squares.)

Pack in an airtight box, or wrap individually in clear cellophane, waxed paper, or foil.

These freeze perfectly and can be served very cold or at room temperature.

NOTES: When you remove the cake from the pan you might see burned and caramelized edges. (You might not—it depends on the pan.) If you do, you can leave them on or cut them off. I have friends who say that this is the best part. I cut them off, but then I can't resist eating them.

These are huge! For some occasions you might want to cut them smaller. They are equally delicious, and sometimes they seem more appropriate.

P.S. Once upon a time . . . I was in the brownie business. I made the original Palm Beach Brownies (without the mints) and sold them to the Jordan Marsh department store here in Miami. I wrapped them individually in clear cellophane and then packaged them in white boxes with clear plastic tops. I wrote the recipe by hand and had it Xeroxed. Each box contained a dozen brownies and the recipe. Business was great, but it took up almost all my time. When I started writing cookbooks, I had to quit the brownie business. But it was great while it lasted.

BALI HAI BROWNIES

I made up these Bali Hai Brownies. I used the above recipe without the walnuts and the mints. I added the following ingredients, just stirred into the dough.

6 ounces crystallized ginger, cut in ¼- to ½-inch pieces (optional)

10 ounces (about 3 packed cups) shredded coconut

10 ounces (2 generous cups) whole macadamia nuts (I used the Mauna Loa nuts that come in a jar—they are roasted and salted.)

The brownies were lush, moist (like thick macaroons), exotic, and dramatic (the whole macadamias were startling). The recipe is extravagant—the ingredients are expensive. The brownies are extraordinary.

CHEESECAKE BROWNIES

Nicole Kaplan of the Institute of Culinary Education

One of my most memorable birthday gifts was a private class with pastry chef Kaplan. She taught me many useful baking techniques. We made this extraordinary dessert—the perfect mix of two classics, fudgy chocolate and rich cheesecake. · MAKES ABOUT 36 SMALL BROWNIES

CHOCOLATE LAYER

4 ounces (1 stick) unsalted butter

6 ounces semisweet chocolate

2 ounces unsweetened chocolate

½ cup packed light brown sugar

¾ cup granulated sugar

3 large eggs

½ cup cake flour

Line a 9-inch square baking pan with parchment paper.

In the top of a double boiler, melt the butter, semisweet chocolate, unsweetened chocolate, and brown sugar. Off the heat, stir in the granulated sugar, eggs, and cake flour. Pour the batter into the prepared pan and spread evenly. Freeze for several hours or up to 1 week.

CREAM CHEESE LAYER

1½ pounds cream cheese

½ cup granulated sugar

3 large eggs

2 ounces semisweet chocolate, melted

Preheat the oven to 325°F.

In the bowl of a stand mixer fitted with the paddle attachment, cream together the cream cheese and sugar. Add the eggs and mix.

Spread the cream cheese mixture on top of the frozen brownies. Drizzle the melted chocolate on top, and swirl to make a decorative pattern. Bake for about 40 minutes, or until the top is set and lightly brown. Cool for a few minutes in the pan. Place in the freezer for 20 minutes before cutting. Slice with a hot, dry knife.

CHUMLEYS

Tracey Zabar

Blondies are in the brownie family, but they contain brown sugar instead of chocolate, which gives them an appealing caramel flavor. In my house, they are called Chumleys, named after a favorite cartoon character—the adorable walrus in *Tennessee Tuxedo and His Tales*. · MAKES 16 SQUARES

1½ cups pecan halves
8 ounces (2 sticks) unsalted butter
2 cups packed light brown sugar
2 large eggs
1 tablespoon pure vanilla extract
2 cups all-purpose flour

2 teaspoons baking powder
½ teaspoon salt
12 ounces (2 cups) bittersweet
chocolate chips (I use the large
Ghirardelli 70 percent bittersweet
chocolate chips)

Preheat the oven to 350°F. Line a half-sheet pan and an 8-inch square baking pan with parchment paper.

Spread the pecans in a single layer on the prepared half-sheet pan. Bake for 6 to 8 minutes, or until the nuts are lightly browned and fragrant. Cool completely on the pan.

Melt the butter in a small saucepan. Place the brown sugar in the bowl of a stand mixer fitted with the paddle attachment. Pour the hot butter over the sugar, and mix. Add the eggs and vanilla, and mix. Add the flour, baking powder, and salt, and mix just until combined. With a silicone spatula, stir in the cooled pecans and chocolate chips.

Spread the batter evenly in the prepared pan and smooth the top. Bake for about 45 minutes, or until the edges start to brown. Cool completely on a wire rack. Wrap in plastic wrap and place in the refrigerator for about 30 minutes, then cut into 2-inch squares.

FIG SQUARES

Karen DeMasco of Locanda Verde

One of pastry chef DeMasco's weaknesses is Fig Newtons. With the addition of wine and black pepper, her version is a bit more grown-up. I am a huge fan of these cookies because they are reminiscent of one of my favorite desserts—the fig squares offered at the Italian bakeries of my childhood. · MAKES 20 SQUARES

FILLING

12 ounces dried figs (about 14 figs)

½ cup honey

1½ cups white wine

¾ teaspoon ground cinnamon

¼ teaspoon freshly ground black
  pepper

½ teaspoon kosher salt

2 tablespoons granulated sugar

Cut the stems off the tops of the figs and cut each fig into 4 pieces.

Combine the honey, wine, cinnamon, pepper, salt, and sugar in a large saucepan. Add the figs, and cook over low heat for about 10 minutes, until they soften. Carefully pour the hot fig mixture into a blender and puree until smooth. Set aside.

DOUGH

8 ounces (2 sticks) unsalted butter,
  softened

½ cup granulated sugar

¼ teaspoon pure vanilla extract

1 large egg

1 large egg yolk

Finely grated zest of ½ lemon

2½ cups all-purpose flour

½ teaspoon kosher salt

In the bowl of a stand mixer fitted with the paddle attachment, combine the butter, sugar, and vanilla. Mix on medium speed until well combined. Add the egg, egg yolk, and lemon zest. Once well mixed, add the flour and salt.

Form the dough into a thin disk, wrap it with plastic wrap, and chill it in the refrigerator for 1 hour until firm.

Preheat the oven to 350°F. Butter an 8 by 10-inch baking pan and line the bottom with parchment paper.

Divide the dough into 2 equal pieces. Roll out 1 piece slightly larger than your pan. Roll the dough over a rolling pin. Center the rolling pin over the pan and unroll the dough, fitting it into the pan so that the entire bottom is covered and about ½ inch rises up the sides.

Spread the fig mixture evenly over the dough.

Roll out the remaining dough and place it atop the fig mixture. Trim the edges so they just meet the sides of the pan. Bake for 40 to 50 minutes, turning the pan halfway through baking, until golden and firm to the touch. Cool completely on a wire rack.

Flip onto a cutting board and cut into 2-inch squares.

LAMINGTON BARS
Shaun Hergatt of SHO Shaun Hergatt

The Lamington is a "true" Aussie icon. One bite brings Chef Hergatt back to his childhood in outback Queensland. These cubes of cake, covered in chocolate ganache and coconut, have a surprise center of raspberry jam. You can either eat them like cookies with your fingers or serve them on individual plates with dessert forks. I love them so much that when the chef asked me how many I wanted for this photograph, I said, "Two thousand." He laughed and sent me a few dozen. • MAKES ABOUT 50 SMALL OR 10 LARGE CUBES

4 large eggs

1 cup granulated sugar

1¾ cups all-purpose flour

1½ teaspoons baking powder

5½ tablespoons unsalted butter

⅓ cup corn syrup

3 tablespoons milk

Preheat the oven to 325°F. Line a half-sheet pan with parchment paper.

In the bowl of a stand mixer fitted with the whisk attachment, beat the eggs and sugar on high speed until light and foamy, about 5 minutes.

In another bowl, sift the flour and baking powder together.

Melt the butter in a small saucepan, and add the corn syrup.

Remove the egg mixture from the mixer. With a silicone spatula, fold in the flour mixture. Add the milk, and then the butter mixture, just until combined. Spread the batter onto the prepared pan. Bake for 8 minutes. Cool completely on a wire rack.

8 ounces milk chocolate, coarsely
    chopped

1 cup heavy cream

Place the chocolate in a heatproof bowl. Heat the cream over a medium heat, just until boiling. Pour the hot cream over the chocolate, stirring until melted and smooth.

FINISH

One 9-ounce jar of raspberry jam

½ pound unsweetened shredded
    coconut

Line a half-sheet pan with parchment paper. Cut the sponge in half, down the middle. Spread the raspberry jam evenly over one half and place the other half on top. Cut into even cubes.

Using a fork, dip each cube into the chocolate ganache, and then roll each one in a bowl of the coconut, coating the entire cube. Place the coated cube on the parchment-lined half-sheet pan. Repeat this process and chill the pan full of cubes, uncovered, in the refrigerator for a few minutes to set.

BACK-TO-SCHOOL RASPBERRY GRANOLA BARS

Karen DeMasco of Locanda Verde

These nutty fruit cookies are perfect for a lunch sack, last-minute bake sale, or early autumn picnic. Crowd-pleasers, they are quick to put together using pantry staples. For a totally different flavor, substitute blackberry jam or your favorite marmalade for the raspberry preserves. · MAKES 16 BARS

6 ounces (1½ sticks) unsalted butter, softened, plus more for the pan

1 cup pecans, roughly chopped

1½ cups unbleached all-purpose flour

1¼ cups old-fashioned rolled oats (not instant)

⅓ cup granulated sugar

⅓ cup packed dark brown sugar

1 teaspoon kosher salt

½ teaspoon baking soda

1 cup raspberry preserves

Preheat the oven to 350°F. Butter an 8-inch square pan and line the bottom with parchment paper. Also, line a half-sheet pan with parchment paper.

Melt the butter in a small saucepan. Remove from the heat and let cool to room temperature.

Spread the pecans in a single layer on the prepared half-sheet pan. Bake for about 5 minutes, or until lightly golden and fragrant. Cool completely on the pan.

In a large bowl, whisk together the flour, oats, granulated sugar, brown sugar, salt, baking soda, and pecans. Pour in the melted butter, and using a wooden spoon, mix together until well combined. Transfer about two-thirds of the dough to the prepared pan. Press the dough evenly into the pan, forming a packed layer.

Using an offset or silicone spatula, spread the preserves over the dough. Evenly sprinkle the remaining dough over the preserves. Bake for about 40 minutes, rotating the pan halfway through, until the top is golden brown and fragrant. Transfer the pan to a wire rack and let it cool completely. Then cut into 2-inch squares.

The bars can be kept in an airtight container at room temperature for up to 1 week.

JAM BARS
Substitute 1 cup of any other flavor preserves for the raspberry preserves.

WHOOPIE PIES

Tracey Zabar

Whoopie pies have been made in New England since the mid-1920s. This version is from a family friend who taught me to make them when I was a little girl. Many years later, I met an Amish quilter from Indiana who shared a very similar recipe. She called the cookies gobs, but her cousins in Pennsylvania and Ohio called them hucklebucks. According to folklore, people would shout "Whoopie!" when they found these treats in their packed lunches. The sweet, gooey filling is the perfect complement for the dry, cakey cookies—reminiscent of a homemade Devil Dog.

• MAKES ABOUT 12 LARGE OR 50 SMALL SANDWICH COOKIES

1 cup granulated sugar

4 ounces (1 stick) unsalted butter, softened

1 teaspoon pure vanilla extract

1 large egg

1 cup milk

2 cups all-purpose flour

¼ teaspoon salt

½ cup Dutch-process cocoa powder, sifted

1½ teaspoons baking soda

½ teaspoon baking powder

Preheat the oven to 425°F. Line two half-sheet pans with parchment paper.

In the bowl of a stand mixer fitted with the paddle attachment, cream the sugar and butter. Add the vanilla, egg, and milk and beat well. Add the flour, salt, cocoa, baking soda, and baking powder, and mix just until combined.

For large cookies, drop by tablespoons onto the prepared pans. For tiny cookies, fill a pastry bag fitted with a large round tip (such as Ateco #807) and pipe 2-inch rounds onto the prepared pans. Space cookies 2 inches apart. Bake for 7 to 9 minutes. Cool completely on wire racks before filling.

6 ounces (1½ sticks) unsalted butter, softened

1½ cups Marshmallow Fluff

¾ teaspoon pure vanilla extract

1½ cups confectioners' sugar, sifted

Heavy cream, as needed

In the bowl of a stand mixer fitted with the whip attachment, beat the butter, Marshmallow Fluff, and vanilla until creamy. Add the confectioners' sugar, a little at a time, and beat until combined. If the mixture is too thick, add a few drops of heavy cream.

Pipe or spoon the filling onto the flat side of a cookie, and sandwich with another cookie. Repeat, making sandwiches with the remaining cookies.

RED VELVET WHOOPIE PIES

John Fraser of Dovetail

Chef Fraser and his pastry chef, Vera, are lovers of all things red velvet, and they make many variations of this type of dessert, even macaroons. They developed these yummy whoopie pies specifically for this book.

• MAKES ABOUT 28 SANDWICH COOKIES

1 cup all-purpose flour
6 tablespoons Dutch-process cocoa
   powder
¼ teaspoon baking powder
½ teaspoon baking soda
½ teaspoon salt

2 tablespoons unsalted butter,
   softened
½ cup packed dark brown sugar
2 tablespoons vegetable oil
1 large egg
½ cup buttermilk
1 tablespoon red food coloring

Preheat the oven to 350°F. Line two half-sheet pans with parchment paper.

Sift together the flour, cocoa powder, baking powder, baking soda, and salt into a bowl, and set aside.

In the bowl of a stand mixer fitted with the paddle attachment, cream the butter, brown sugar, and oil until light and fluffy. Add the egg and mix until well incorporated. Add the flour mixture, alternating with the buttermilk and food coloring, in three additions.

Fill a pastry bag with a plain tip (such as Ateco #806) and pipe rounds about 1½ inches in diameter onto the prepared pans, leaving a 1-inch space between cookies. Bake for 6 to 9 minutes, or until a cookie springs back slightly when pressed in the center. Cool completely on wire racks before filling.

CREAM CHEESE FILLING

2 ounces (½ stick) unsalted butter,
softened

½ cup cream cheese, cold

1 cup confectioners' sugar

½ teaspoon pure vanilla extract

In the bowl of a stand mixer fitted with the paddle attachment, cream the butter and cream cheese until smooth. Beat in the sugar and vanilla.

Spread or pipe the filling between 2 cookies, and repeat with the remaining cookies. Serve immediately.

LAUREN'S SNICKERDOODLES

Alex Stupak of wd-50

Chef Stupak—whose wife, Lauren Resler, is a pastry chef—sent me a note along with this tempting recipe. "Lauren loves snickerdoodles. I had never even heard of this cookie before meeting her. One day I took her recipe and replaced the cinnamon with the Mexican variety, which has a unique and interesting flavor. I make them often for our staff meal at wd-50, which gives me the opportunity to sneak some home." • MAKES ABOUT 45 COOKIES

8 ounces (2 sticks) unsalted butter, softened

1½ cups packed light brown sugar

2 large eggs

2¾ cups all-purpose flour

2 teaspoons cream of tartar

1 teaspoon baking soda

¼ teaspoon salt

¼ cup granulated sugar

2 teaspoons ground Mexican cinnamon

Line two half-sheet pans with parchment paper.

In the bowl of a stand mixer fitted with the paddle attachment, cream the butter and brown sugar, beating on high speed until light. Add the eggs, one at a time. Scrape the sides of the bowl and add the flour, cream of tartar, baking soda, and salt, and mix just until incorporated.

Scoop the dough into 1¼-inch balls and place them on the prepared pans. Loosely cover each pan with plastic wrap, and freeze the balls for 6 hours.

Preheat the oven to 350°F.

In a small bowl, mix the granulated sugar and cinnamon.

Roll the dough balls in the cinnamon-sugar mixture. Place them 2 inches apart on the prepared pans. Bake for 8 to 10 minutes, until set. Cool completely on wire racks.

SNICKERDOODLES

Tom Valenti of Ouest

There are many theories about the origin of the name snickerdoodles. Some believe that the name is from the German or Dutch words *schnecke* or *sneckrad*, meaning "snail," while others think it is just a whimsical title. Regardless of its origins, Chef Valenti finds the name "irresistible" and offers "a relatively low-sugar version of the popular sugar-and-cinnamon-dusted cookies. They keep well enough that you can also pack, wrap, and give them out as gifts during the holidays." · MAKES ABOUT 30 COOKIES

1¼ cups plus 2 tablespoons all-purpose flour

¼ cup plus 3 tablespoons granulated sugar, divided

1 teaspoon cream of tartar

½ teaspoon baking powder

Pinch of coarse salt

4 ounces (1 stick) unsalted butter, softened

1 large egg

1 tablespoon ground cinnamon

Preheat the oven to 350°F. Line a half-sheet pan with parchment paper.

Put the flour, ¼ cup plus 2 tablespoons of the sugar, cream of tartar, baking powder, and salt in a bowl, and mix them together.

Put the butter in a large bowl and beat on high with an electric mixer until it is light in color and fluffy. Reduce the speed of the mixer, add the egg, and beat until incorporated. Add the dry ingredients to the bowl and beat on medium speed until a dough forms.

Shape the dough into balls about the size of a chestnut and arrange them on the prepared pan about 1 inch apart.

Mix the remaining 1 tablespoon of sugar and the cinnamon together in a small bowl. Lightly sprinkle the sugar mixture over the balls of dough. Bake the cookies until the balls flatten a bit and turn nicely golden, about 20 minutes. Cool completely on wire racks.

MADELEINES FOR ALEX

Nicole Kaplan of the Institute of Culinary Education

Pastry chef Kaplan recently began making these divine, classic cakey cookies. She explains, "My oldest son fell madly for madeleines one night when we went out to dinner. They were served warm, right out of the oven, and he was so taken he ate the whole basket, overlooking all the other fancy and wonderful desserts. He asks for them all the time, but won't accept any store-bought imitations, so our madeleine pan is kept floured and at the ready in the freezer in case the urge hits." · MAKES ABOUT 24 MADELEINES

6 tablespoons granulated sugar

1 tablespoon dark brown sugar

Pinch of salt

⅔ cup all-purpose flour

1 teaspoon baking powder

Seeds scraped from 1 vanilla bean

Grated zest of 1 lemon

2 large eggs

3 ounces (¾ stick) unsalted butter, melted

Butter and flour madeleine molds, and place in the freezer overnight.

In the bowl of a stand mixer fitted with the paddle attachment, mix the granulated sugar, brown sugar, salt, flour, baking powder, vanilla seeds, and lemon zest. Add the eggs, one at a time, to combine. Add the melted butter. Cover the bowl with plastic wrap and refrigerate overnight to rest. This improves the quality of the rise.

Preheat the oven to 325°F.

Pipe the batter two-thirds full into the prepared madeleine molds. Bake immediately. The madeleines are done in 8 to 10 minutes, or when they have risen with a nice hump in the middle and are dry to the touch. Remove the madeleines from the molds while still warm. Cool completely on wire racks.

RICOTTA COOKIES

Dale Colantropo Fitzgerald

My lifelong friend Dale always shared her grandmothers, Serafina and Rose, with me. She recounted this loving tale of the bakers of these traditional Italian cookies. "Serafina chauffeured all the neighborhood Sicilian ladies to church every day. Wearing their black dresses, they piled into Fifi, our dark-green-with-plaid-interior 1956 Ford—often with yours truly stuffed between them. The grammies grew all of our fruits and vegetables in the backyard. We lived beside the town cemetery, and everyone visited the graves of loved ones, so we always had company at the picnic table under our grape arbor. My passion for cooking comes from them. I like to say I attended the Culinary Institute of My Italian Grandmothers." This is their cookie. • MAKES 60 TO 70 COOKIES

3 cups cake flour

1 cup sifted all-purpose flour

1 teaspoon baking powder

1 teaspoon baking soda

8 ounces (2 sticks) unsalted butter, softened

2 cups granulated sugar

2 large eggs, lightly beaten

2 teaspoons pure vanilla extract

One 15-ounce container ricotta cheese (part skim or whole milk)

Preheat the oven to 350°F. Line two half-sheet pans with parchment paper.

Combine cake flour, all-purpose flour, baking powder, and baking soda in a medium bowl. Set aside.

In the bowl of a stand mixer fitted with the paddle attachment, cream the butter with the sugar, then add the eggs. In a medium bowl, combine the vanilla and ricotta. Alternate adding the ricotta and the flour mixture to the butter mixture, creating a fairly thick batter.

Drop the batter by teaspoonfuls onto the prepared pans, 12 on each pan. Bake for about 8 minutes, or until the bottoms of the cookies are lightly golden. The tops will not brown. Repeat with the remaining batter, baking 12 on each pan. Cool completely on wire racks.

One 1-pound box confectioners' sugar
½ cup half-and-half
1 tablespoon grated lemon zest
Juice of 1 fresh lemon

½ teaspoon pure vanilla, orange, or
anise extract (optional)
Few drops food coloring (optional)
Colored sugar or sprinkles (optional)

Combine the confectioners' sugar, half-and-half, lemon zest, lemon juice, vanilla (if using), and food coloring (if using), and beat until gloriously creamy and thick.

Dip the top of each cookie into the glaze, dust with sugar or sprinkles (if using), and return to the rack or place in the refrigerator to set the glaze.

These cookies freeze well unglazed. Defrost and glaze as needed.

RICOTTA CHIP COOKIES
Omit the glaze. Add ½ cup mini dark chocolate chips to the batter.

RICOTTA SAMMIES
Spread your favorite fruit preserves, lemon curd, or Nutella on one cookie, and top with another. Dust with confectioners' sugar.

RICOTTA COCONUT CLOUDS
Omit lemon from the glaze. Glaze the cookie tops, and immediately dip in freshly grated coconut.

PINEAPPLE TEA CAKES

François Payard of François Payard Bakery

These elegant tea cakes are as pleasurable to make as they are to eat. Chef Payard says, "Each small cake is garnished with a piece of pineapple, but I've also made raisin tea cakes with raisins soaked in rum instead of the pineapple. Be sure to use almond paste, not marzipan, which is made from more or less the same ingredients but, unlike the paste, is cooked. You could replace the preserves with apricot marmalade." For these petits fours, you will need the following special equipment: one hundred 1-inch paper petit four cups and a pastry bag fitted with a ¼-inch plain tip (such as Ateco #2). • MAKES ABOUT 100 PETITS FOURS

1 pound, 10 ounces almond paste

2 tablespoons apricot preserves

5 large eggs

3 large egg yolks

½ cup plus 1 tablespoon all-purpose flour

7 ounces (1¾ sticks) unsalted butter, melted

1 pineapple, peeled, quartered, cored, and cut into ¼-inch cubes

2 tablespoons confectioners' sugar

Preheat the oven to 350°F. Arrange one hundred 1-inch paper petit four cups on a half-sheet pan.

In an electric mixer fitted with a paddle attachment, combine the almond paste and apricot preserves and beat at medium speed until smooth. Beat in the eggs, one at a time, mixing until each egg is incorporated before adding the next. Beat in the egg yolks, one at a time. Beat in the flour at low speed. Add the melted butter and mix until blended.

Fill a pastry bag fitted with a ¼-inch plain tip with the batter. Pipe the batter into the paper cups, filling them three-quarters full. Place a cube of pineapple on top of each cup. Sift the confectioners' sugar over the cups.

Bake the cakes for 25 to 28 minutes, or until light golden brown. Let cool on the half-sheet pan.

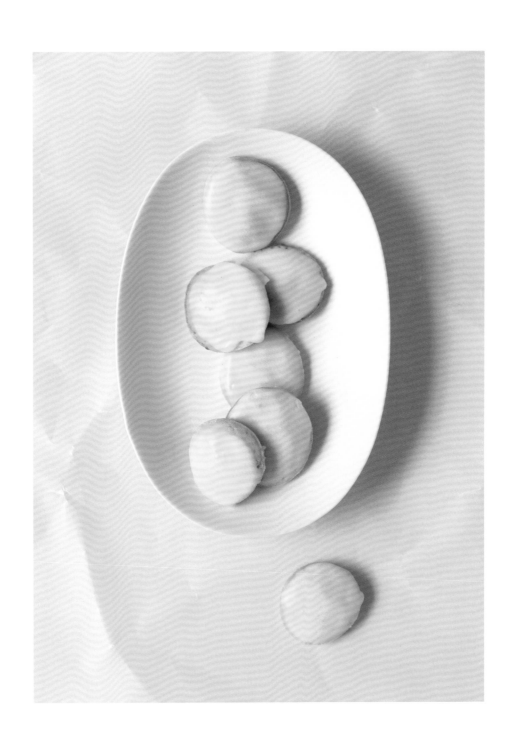

ORANGE COOKIES

Lidia Bastianich of Lidia's Italy

These fragrant, citrusy cookies with a sweet glaze hit the spot at the end of a meal. Chef Bastianich writes, "These traditional Italian cookies are as easy as it gets, and everybody loves them. The citrus flavoring makes them particularly inviting. Most likely, you have had them at Italian family celebrations like weddings, confirmations, and baptisms. Not too sweet, these cookies keep for a week or two in a cookie container." · MAKES ABOUT 80 COOKIES

3 cups all-purpose flour
2 teaspoons baking powder
¼ teaspoon salt
6 ounces (1½ sticks) unsalted butter, softened
½ cup plus 1 tablespoon granulated sugar

3 large eggs
1 teaspoon pure vanilla extract
2 tablespoons fresh orange juice
2 tablespoons fresh lemon juice
1 tablespoon grated orange zest

Sift together the flour, baking powder, and salt into a large bowl, and set aside.

In the bowl of a stand mixer fitted with the paddle attachment, cream the butter and sugar on medium speed until light and fluffy, about 2 minutes. Add the eggs, one at a time, beating well between additions. Add the vanilla, orange juice, lemon juice, and orange zest. Beat to combine. With the mixer off, add the flour mixture and mix just until combined. Wrap the dough in plastic wrap and let it rest in the refrigerator for 1 hour.

Roll the dough into 4 logs, each about 1½ inches in diameter and 10 to 12 inches long. Chill or freeze the logs, uncovered, until firm enough to cut without losing their shape.

Preheat the oven to 350°F. Line three half-sheet pans with parchment paper.

Cut the logs into ½-inch rounds and place on the prepared pans. Bake for about 15 minutes, or until the cookies are golden. Cool completely on wire racks.

2½ cups confectioners' sugar   ¼ cup fresh orange juice, or as needed

Sift the confectioners' sugar into a bowl and whisk in the orange juice to make a smooth glaze.

Dip a cookie in the glaze, which should form a thin layer. If necessary, adjust the consistency of the glaze with more juice or confectioners' sugar. Repeat the dipping process, and then let the glazed cookies set on wire racks.

CHAPTER

No. **2**

NUTS, CHIPS,

AND

OATMEAL COOKIES

ALMOND *KIPFERL*

Kurt Gutenbrunner of Wallsé

A variation of the popular Austrian holiday cookie called vanilla *kipferl*, these almond-flavored crescent cookies are absolutely delicious and easy to make. Chef Gutenbrunner likes to serve them as petits fours, a sweet finishing touch, after a special meal. • MAKES ABOUT 16 COOKIES

8 ounces (2 sticks) unsalted butter, softened

1 cup confectioners' sugar, divided

3 large egg yolks

1½ teaspoons pure vanilla extract

½ teaspoon salt

1¾ cups all-purpose flour

¾ cup raw almonds, finely ground

Preheat the oven to 325°F. Line one half-sheet pan with parchment paper.

In the bowl of a stand mixer fitted with the paddle attachment, cream the butter with ½ cup of the confectioners' sugar at medium-high speed until pale and fluffy, about 1 minute. Add the egg yolks, vanilla, and salt and beat at medium-high speed until blended, scraping the sides of the bowl as needed. Beat in the flour and ground almonds at slow speed until just incorporated. Cover the dough with plastic wrap and refrigerate until firm, at least 30 minutes.

Using about 1½ tablespoons of the dough for each cookie, roll the dough into 3-inch-long cylinders with tapered ends. Form the cookies into crescents and transfer them to the prepared pan, spacing them 1 inch apart.

Bake the cookies for 18 minutes, or until light golden. Cool on the pans for 10 minutes, or until just cool enough to handle.

Using a fine sieve, sprinkle the remaining ½ cup confectioners' sugar over the cookies.

SUGAR'S HUNGARIAN CRESCENTS

Angela Pinkerton of Eleven Madison Park

Chef Pinkerton adapted her old family friend Sugar's recipe, which is the only one in the book that uses yeast. Although the recipe looks complicated, it is easy to prepare this lovely cookie. The dough can be made in minutes and is left in the refrigerator overnight to rise slowly. The next day, you can quickly whip up the filling, assemble, and bake. · MAKES ABOUT 72 COOKIES

½ cup crème fraîche

½ cake fresh yeast or 1 teaspoon
   active dry yeast

8 ounces (2 sticks) unsalted butter,
   softened

1 large egg

1 large egg yolk

Seeds scraped from ½ vanilla bean

3 cups all-purpose flour, sifted

In the bowl of a stand mixer fitted with the paddle attachment, combine the crème fraîche and the yeast. Mix in the butter, egg, egg yolk, and vanilla seeds. Add the flour and combine well.

    Roll the dough into walnut-size balls, cover, and refrigerate overnight. (The dough can also be frozen for later use.)

FILLING

4 ounces almond paste

Seeds scraped from ½ vanilla bean

Grated zest of ½ lemon

¼ teaspoon ground cinnamon

¼ cup granulated sugar

1 large egg yolk

Fresh lemon juice, as needed

The next day, make the filling. Mix the almond paste with the vanilla seeds, lemon zest, and cinnamon in a bowl. Add the sugar, and then the egg yolk. Add lemon juice as needed to get a spreadable consistency. (The amount needed will depend on the moisture content of your almond paste.)

2 cups almonds (or walnuts), finely
   chopped
2 large egg whites

Confectioners' sugar for sprinkling
   and dusting

Preheat the oven to 350°F. Line two half-sheet pans with parchment paper.

Place the almonds in a small bowl, and set aside. Place the egg whites in another small bowl, and set aside.

Take 3 balls of dough out of the refrigerator at a time and cut each one in half. Sprinkle confectioners' sugar on your work surface to prevent the dough from sticking. Using a rolling pin, roll each half ball into a very thin circle. Spread the dough gently with the filling. Roll up and pinch the ends. Dip each one into the egg whites (or use a pastry brush), then roll in the almonds. Shape into a crescent. Place on prepared pans and repeat with the remaining dough. Before baking, chill in the refrigerator for 10 minutes.

Bake for 12 to 15 minutes, or until lightly golden brown. Cool completely on wire racks. Dust with sifted confectioners' sugar.

CRESCENTS OF ALMOND AND CARDAMOM

Isra Gordon of the French Culinary Institute

Put sugar, almonds, and cardamom together and what you get is a cookie not only for the holiday season, but also for any guest you want to impress. This crescent spices up any event. Chef Gordon remembers visiting her grandmother back home in Grenada, where there always was a jar filled with these tender cookies for the children. Interested in learning how to make them, she developed a passion for shortbreads. But over time, her love for spices, nuts, and fruits led her to add these tastes to her baking experiments. She liked the results, and after trying out a few different combinations, this one stood out as the favorite.

• MAKES ABOUT 40 COOKIES

4 ounces (1 stick) unsalted butter, chilled and cubed

¾ cup turbinado sugar

1 large egg

½ cup ground almonds (or almond flour)

2½ cups all-purpose flour, sifted

1 teaspoon baking powder

½ teaspoon ground cardamom

2 tablespoons candied orange peel

½ cup dried apricots, coarsely chopped

¼ teaspoon pure almond extract

1 large egg white

½ cup sliced blanched almonds

Granulated sugar for sprinkling

Preheat the oven to 350°F. Line two half-sheet pans with parchment paper.

In the bowl of a stand mixer fitted with the paddle attachment, cream the butter and sugar. Add the egg until combined. Add the ground almonds, flour, baking powder, and cardamom. Fold in the orange peel, apricots, and almond extract. If the batter is too dry, add a little water.

(If using a food processor: Combine the butter and flour in the work bowl of a food processor and pulse. Add the sugar, ground almonds, baking powder, and cardamom and pulse. Add the egg and almond extract and pulse. If the batter is too dry, add a little water. Turn the batter out into a mixing bowl and, with a silicone spatula, add the orange peel and apricots.)

Form the dough into a disk and wrap in plastic wrap. Chill in the refrigerator for 20 minutes.

Cut the chilled dough into 40 small pieces. Roll out each piece into a small cylinder, and pinch into crescent shapes, brush with the egg white, and sprinkle the almonds and sugar on top. Place on the prepared pans. Bake for about 15 minutes, or until light golden brown. Cool completely on wire racks.

MELOMAKARONA

Michelle Tampakis of the Institute of Culinary Education

Chef Tampakis shared this traditional Greek recipe for honey-dipped walnut cookies. During the fasting periods preceding Easter and Christmas, when eggs and dairy products are avoided, a vegetable spread such as olive *fytini* is substituted for the butter. · MAKES ABOUT 70 COOKIES

9 ounces vegetable oil

3 ounces (¾ stick) unsalted butter, softened

¾ cup sparkling water

1 cup granulated sugar

1 tablespoon ground nutmeg

Grated zest of 1 orange

8 cups all-purpose flour

1½ teaspoons baking soda

1½ teaspoons baking powder

1 teaspoon salt

Preheat the oven to 300°F. Line two half-sheet pans with parchment paper.

In the bowl of a stand mixer fitted with the paddle attachment, combine the oil, butter, sparkling water, sugar, nutmeg, and orange zest, and beat until smooth. Sift together the flour, baking soda, baking powder, and salt. Add the flour mixture to the oil mixture, combining just until a dough forms.

Divide the dough into 1½-ounce pieces (each about 1 rounded tablespoonful). Shape the cookies into ovals and place on the prepared pans. Bake for about 40 minutes, or until golden brown. Cool completely on wire racks.

SYRUP

1½ cups granulated sugar

1½ cups honey

1 cup water

1 cup finely chopped walnuts (optional)

Combine the sugar, honey, and water in a medium saucepan. Bring to a boil, and boil for 3 minutes. Skim any foam that forms on the surface. Allow the syrup to cool. Dip the cookies in the syrup and sprinkle with walnuts (if using).

FLORENTINE COOKIES

Marc Aumont of The Modern

Chef Aumont made these cookies when he apprenticed in his father's chocolate and pastry shop in the French resort of Chamonix Mont Blanc. Quite different from the Florentines that most people know, these have a nice combination of flavors. These cookies are very close to candy. The preferred ingredients are cubes of orange and melon confit (fruit preserved in sugar), but they are often unavailable in America, even at fancy food stores. Candied and dried fruit, coarsely chopped, is a great substitute. Do not be intimidated if you are unfamiliar with entremet rings. They are easy to use, as are the less expensive but not as durable English muffin rings. · MAKES ABOUT 8 LARGE COOKIES

½ cup candied orange peel, diced, or
    orange confit cubes
½ cup dried cherries or pineapple,
    diced, or melon confit cubes
1 cup sliced almonds
¼ cup pastry flour

½ cup heavy cream
½ cup granulated sugar
1 tablespoon honey
4 ounces bittersweet or semisweet
    chocolate (optional)

Preheat the oven to 300°F. Line a half-sheet pan with parchment paper and lay eight 3-inch entremet rings (or five 3¾-inch English muffin rings) on top of the parchment-lined pan.

Mix the orange peel, cherries, almonds, and pastry flour in a small bowl, and set aside.

In a small saucepan, mix the cream, sugar, and honey and bring to a boil while stirring. Remove the pan from the heat and stir in the fruit mixture.

Scoop the mixture into the rings on the prepared pan. Bake for 14 to 15 minutes, or until the cookies are a light caramel color. Remove the cookies from the rings and transfer to a wire rack to cool.

Melt the chocolate (if using) and dip the back of each cookie into the chocolate. Transfer the cookies to waxed paper while the chocolate hardens.

CASHEW *POLVORONES*

Kir Rodriguez of the French Culinary Institute

Chef Rodriguez's cashew *polvorones* are his childhood favorite. When he was growing up in the green hills of Puerto Rico, his friends' moms all made them. Crowd-pleasers, they are easy to make and totally addictive. These cookies are popular throughout the world, and are also called wedding bells, snowballs, and tea cakes, among other such names. · MAKES ABOUT 40 SMALL COOKIES

½ cup cashews (or any other nut)

¾ cup granulated sugar, divided

8 ounces (2 sticks) unsalted butter, softened

½ teaspoon salt

½ teaspoon pure vanilla extract

1 teaspoon ground cardamom

1¾ cups all-purpose flour

Confectioners' sugar for finishing

Preheat the oven to 300°F. Line two half-sheet pans with parchment paper.

Spread the cashews in a single layer on one of the prepared pans. Bake for 6 to 8 minutes, or until the nuts are slightly browned and fragrant. Cool completely on the pan. Grind the cooled nuts with approximately one-third of the sugar in a food processor. Set the prepared pan aside until it is time to bake the cookies.

In the bowl of a stand mixer fitted with the paddle attachment, cream the butter, salt, and the remaining sugar until very light and fluffy. Add the vanilla and cardamom. Add the ground cashews and flour, and mix well until the dough gathers into a ball. With a silicone spatula, scrape the bowl several times to ensure thorough mixing.

Roll the dough by hand into small balls, approximately 1 inch in diameter, and place on the prepared pans. Bake the cookies for 15 to 20 minutes, or until browned around the edges. Let them cool completely on wire racks. Roll the cookies in confectioners' sugar. You might need to reroll them just before serving.

rt a' retal kebel's par heore kelnek,

egát szikra lölte nixes jelen,

ott röpül mid szellem itt lanáwál,

iffjú hőssel, Isten angyalával?

Czuczor Gergely

ICE-CREAM SANDWICHES

Thomas Keller of Ad Hoc

Making ice-cream sandwiches with these elegant cookies is a modern spin on the traditional hazelnut linzer. Of course, you can substitute raspberry jam for the ice cream. Either way, Chef Keller has elevated this perennial favorite.

• MAKES ABOUT 12 ICE-CREAM SANDWICHES

LINZER COOKIES

1 cup ground peeled hazelnuts

1½ cups all-purpose flour

¼ teaspoon ground cinnamon

½ teaspoon Dutch-process cocoa
   powder

6 ounces (1½ sticks) unsalted butter,
   softened

1 teaspoon grated lemon zest

½ teaspoon fresh lemon juice

¾ cup confectioners' sugar

Whisk together the hazelnuts, flour, cinnamon, and cocoa powder in a medium bowl; set aside.

In the bowl of a stand mixer fitted with the paddle attachment, mix the butter, lemon zest, and lemon juice on medium speed. Add the sugar and beat for 2 to 3 minutes, until light and fluffy. Add the dry ingredients, and mix on low speed to combine, then increase the speed to medium and beat to incorporate, scraping down the sides as necessary.

Transfer the dough to a work surface and form into a 7-inch square. Wrap in plastic wrap and refrigerate for at least 30 minutes, or up to 5 days.

Preheat the oven to 350°F. Line two half-sheet pans with parchment paper.

Cut the dough in half. Roll each piece out between 2 pieces of parchment paper to just under ¼ inch thick. Cut out cookies with a 3-inch square cutter (or any other shape) and transfer to the prepared pans, leaving about 1 inch between them. Bake for 18 to 20 minutes, switching the position and rotating the sheets halfway through, until light golden. Remove the sheets from the oven and cool for 2 to 5 minutes to firm the cookies up. Transfer the cookies directly to the racks to cool completely. (The cookies can be stored in an airtight container for up to 2 days.)

Fill sandwiches with ice cream or raspberry jam.

ICE CREAM

1 quart homemade ice cream, just
spun, or store-bought ice cream,
softened

Line a quarter sheet pan (9 by 13 by 1 inch) with a piece of plastic wrap, leaving an overhang on both long sides. Spread the ice cream in an even layer in the pan. Fold over the plastic and freeze until firm.

To assemble ice-cream sandwiches: Remove the sheet of ice cream from the freezer. Lift up the edges of the plastic to remove the ice cream. Have a bowl of hot water at your side. Using the cutter you used to make the cookies or a knife, cut squares or rounds of ice cream slightly smaller than the cookies, dipping the cutter or knife into the hot water and drying it with a towel before each cut. Assemble the sandwiches and serve immediately, or wrap in plastic wrap and freeze for up to 3 days.

PEANUT BUTTER COOKIES

Marc Murphy of Landmarc

Peanut butter cookies have been Chef Murphy's favorite since he was a kid. He also loves Nutella, which he slathers on everything. Since the first time he spread it on a peanut butter cookie, this chef has never turned back. They are now a big hit, especially with his children.

• MAKES ABOUT 30 SMALL SANDWICH COOKIES

2½ cups all-purpose flour
½ teaspoon baking soda
½ teaspoon baking powder
½ teaspoon salt
8 ounces (2 sticks) butter, softened
1 cup granulated sugar
1 cup packed light brown sugar

1 cup peanut butter (creamy or crunchy)
2 large eggs
2 teaspoons pure vanilla extract
1 cup roasted salted peanuts, finely ground
One 13-ounce jar Nutella

Preheat the oven to 350°F. Line two half-sheet pans with parchment paper.

Sift the flour, baking soda, baking powder, and salt, and set aside.

In the bowl of a stand mixer fitted with the paddle attachment (or by hand), beat the butter until creamy. Add the granulated sugar and brown sugar and mix until fluffy and pale. Beat in the peanut butter, then add the eggs and vanilla. Mix in the flour mixture, along with the ground peanuts.

Using a tablespoon-sized scoop, drop the cookies onto the prepared pans and bake for 10 minutes. Cool completely on wire racks.

Place 1 teaspoon of Nutella in the center of each cookie, and sandwich with another cookie.

MACADAMIA MILK CHOCOLATE-PEPPERMINT COOKIES

Jonathan Waxman of Barbuto

Chef Waxman added a rich chocolate-peppermint cream filling to these delightful, nutty cookies. The unusual flavor combination of macadamia nuts and mint is extremely satisfying. • MAKES ABOUT 35 SANDWICH COOKIES

2 cups crushed raw macadamia nuts
8 ounces (2 sticks) unsalted butter, softened
½ cup granulated sugar

½ cup packed light brown sugar
1½ teaspoons pure vanilla extract
2 cups all-purpose flour
1 teaspoon salt

Preheat the oven to 350°F. Line two half-sheet pans with parchment paper.

Spread the macadamia nuts in a single layer on one of the prepared pans. Bake for 6 to 8 minutes, or until the nuts are lightly browned and fragrant. Cool completely on the pan. Set aside the prepared pan to reuse to bake the cookies.

In the bowl of a stand mixer fitted with the paddle attachment, cream the butter with the granulated sugar and brown sugar. Beat in the vanilla. Add the flour and salt, and mix just until the dough forms. Stir in the macadamia nuts.

Roll out the dough to ⅜ inch thick on waxed or parchment paper. Place in the refrigerator for 1 hour. Remove the dough from the refrigerator and cut with a 1½-inch round cookie cutter. Place the cookies on the prepared pans. Bake for 8 to 10 minutes. Cool completely on wire racks.

FILLING

5 ounces milk chocolate (best quality, such as Green & Black's), chopped
2 ounces bittersweet chocolate, chopped

½ cup heavy cream
½ teaspoon pure peppermint extract
Pinch of salt

Put the milk chocolate and the bittersweet chocolate together in a small bowl. In a small saucepan, scald the cream and then pour it over the chocolate. Add the peppermint and salt, stirring constantly. Cover the bowl with plastic wrap and place in the refrigerator to cool, about 45 minutes.

When the chocolate-peppermint cream filling has thickened, make sandwiches by spreading the filling between 2 cookies.

PECAN DELIGHTS

Michael McCarty of Michael's

With the addition of pecans, these wonderful treats are Chef McCarty's take on the classic butter cookie. Although the recipe calls for very little granulated sugar, the cookies are dusted with confectioners' sugar, making them just sweet enough. · MAKES ABOUT 48 COOKIES

8 ounces (2 sticks) unsalted butter, softened

¼ cup granulated sugar

Pinch of salt

1 cup coarsely chopped pecans

2 cups all-purpose flour

Confectioners' sugar for dusting

Preheat the oven to 350°F. Line two half-sheet pans with parchment paper.

In the bowl of a stand mixer fitted with the paddle attachment, cream the butter and granulated sugar, then beat in the salt and pecans. Reduce the speed to low and gradually blend in the flour.

With a teaspoon or a 1-inch scooper, scoop out small balls of the dough and place them about 1 inch apart on the prepared pans. Bake for 12 to 15 minutes, or until light golden. Cool completely on wire racks. Place the confectioners' sugar in a sifter and shake it over the cookies.

COCONUT CHOCOLATE CHIP COOKIES

Pichet Ong of Spot Dessert Bar

Chef Ong created a sophisticated version of the perennial chocolate chip favorite when he was the pastry chef at New York City's Spice Market restaurant. The staff loved these cookies so much that whenever the chef prepared pretty packages of them for diners to take home, some of the treats would disappear from the kitchen. · MAKES ABOUT 36 COOKIES

1⅓ cups unsweetened finely shredded coconut

2 cups all-purpose flour

1½ teaspoons baking powder

8 ounces (2 sticks) unsalted butter, softened

¾ cup plus 1 tablespoon granulated sugar

1 cup packed dark brown sugar

½ teaspoon salt

2 large eggs

2 teaspoons pure vanilla extract

3 cups chocolate *pistoles* (66 percent to 72 percent chocolate), roughly chopped

Preheat the oven to 300°F.

Spread the coconut on a half-sheet pan, lined with parchment paper, and bake until golden brown and fragrant, 7 minutes. Turn the oven off and set the pan aside to cool completely.

Sift together the flour and baking powder, and set aside. Put the butter, granulated sugar, brown sugar, salt, and cooled toasted coconut into the bowl of a stand mixer fitted with the paddle attachment. Mix on medium speed until the mixture is light and fluffy, 3 minutes. With the machine running, add the eggs, one at a time, and the vanilla.

Turn the mixer speed to low and add half the flour mixture. When incorporated, add the remaining flour and mix until no traces of flour remain. Stir in the chocolate chips. (You can also make the dough by hand. Stir the ingredients in the order above.) If you have time, cover and chill for at least 2 hours or up to 3 days before baking.

Preheat the oven to 325°F and line two half-sheet pans with parchment paper. Scoop the cookie dough into 1-inch balls and place them 2 inches apart on the prepared pans. Bake until brown and crisp, 12 minutes. Cool on wire racks, and serve immediately or store in an airtight container for up to 3 days.

NOTE: Creaming the butter with the coconut maximizes the cookies' distinctive nuttiness, which provides a great backdrop for the rich, deep flavor of the bittersweet chocolate. Be sure to use unsweetened coconut—not only does it taste much better than the sweetened variety, it also makes these cookies crumbly and crisp. Instead of chocolate chips, which are coated to prevent them from melting and losing their shape, use *couverture* chocolates because they blend into the dough as it bakes. Think of this creation as a chocolate "lava" cookie.

MONSTER COOKIES

Nancy Olson of Gramercy Tavern

Chef Olson's flourless cookies are big—and not just for kids. The sweets aficionado in your life will love the wonderful combination of candy, chocolate, and oatmeal mixed in a peanut butter monster. · MAKES ABOUT 21 COOKIES

4 ounces (1 stick) unsalted butter, softened

1 cup granulated sugar

1 cup packed light brown sugar

1 tablespoon corn syrup

12 ounces creamy peanut butter

1½ teaspoons pure vanilla extract

3 large eggs

2 teaspoons baking soda

4½ cups old-fashioned rolled oats (not instant)

⅔ cup M&M's

⅔ cup semisweet chocolate chips

Line four half-sheet pans with parchment paper.

In the bowl of a stand mixer fitted with the paddle attachment, cream the butter, granulated sugar, and brown sugar. Add the corn syrup, peanut butter, and vanilla. Beat in the eggs, one at a time, then add the baking soda and oats. Fold in the M&M's and chocolate chips.

Using a large #16 scoop, drop the dough onto the prepared pans. Refrigerate the dough overnight.

Preheat the oven to 325°F.

Remove the pans from the refrigerator. Bake for 17 to 20 minutes, or just until they start to brown at the edges. It is important to underbake these cookies. Cool completely on wire racks.

SANDYS

Tracey Zabar

These teatime treats, named in honor of my friend and longtime editor, are sweet and indeed quite sandy, with their surprising hint of cinnamon. The addition of candied citrus peel (if using) adds another unusual taste and texture to the cookies. • MAKES ABOUT 40 SMALL COOKIES

4 ounces (1 stick) unsalted butter,
   softened
½ cup granulated sugar
1 large egg
1½ teaspoons pure vanilla extract
½ teaspoon salt

½ teaspoon ground cinnamon
1¼ cups all-purpose flour
12 ounces (2 cups) bittersweet or
   semisweet chocolate chips
½ cup candied orange or lemon peel,
   coarsely chopped (optional)

Preheat the oven to 350°F. Line two half-sheet pans with parchment paper.

In the bowl of a stand mixer fitted with the paddle attachment, cream the butter with the sugar. Add the egg and vanilla and mix. Add the salt, cinnamon, and flour, and beat just until combined. With a silicone spatula, fold in the chocolate chips and the peel (if using).

Drop by rounded tablespoons onto the prepared pans. Bake for 10 to 12 minutes, or until lightly browned around the edges. Cool completely on wire racks.

CHERRY SURPRISE COOKIES

David Zabar of Zabar's

cookies, these are packed with dried cherries
abar makes them whenever he wants some-
nakes a small batch—double the ingredients if

ABOUT 30 COOKIES

½ teaspoon baking soda

1¼ cups all-purpose flour

½ cup dried cherries

¼ cup candied orange peel, coarsely
    chopped

¼ cup semisweet chocolate chips

wo half-sheet pans with parchment paper.
· fitted with the paddle attachment, cream the
wn sugar. Add the egg and vanilla. Mix in the
until combined. With a silicone spatula, gently
and chocolate chips.
unded tablespoon, drop the cookies onto the
minutes, or until the cookies are golden brown.
Cool completely on wire racks.

TODD'S FAVORITE TRIPLE CHOCOLATE AND WALNUT COOKIES

Todd English of Olives

Chef English came up with this recipe for his three kids—Oliver, Isabelle, and Simon—because each of them wanted different-flavored chips—semisweet, milk, and white chocolate, in addition to peanut butter. To make everyone happy, he put all of them in the batter and added his favorite ingredient, walnuts. These cookies are the perfect combo of salty and sweet.

• MAKES ABOUT 36 COOKIES

8 ounces (2 sticks) unsalted butter, softened

1 cup granulated sugar

1 cup packed light brown sugar

2 large eggs

2 teaspoons pure vanilla extract

3 cups all-purpose flour

1 teaspoon baking soda

¼ teaspoon baking powder

1 teaspoon salt

1½ cups semisweet chocolate chips

½ cup milk chocolate chips

½ cup white chocolate chips

¼ cup peanut butter chips (optional)

½ cup walnuts, roughly chopped

Preheat the oven to 350°F. Set out three ungreased half-sheet pans.

In the bowl of a stand mixer fitted with the paddle attachment, cream together the butter, granulated sugar, and brown sugar until smooth. Beat in the eggs, one at a time, then stir in the vanilla. Combine the flour, baking soda, baking powder, and salt. Add the flour mixture to the batter, and mix until incorporated. With a silicone spatula, fold in the semisweet, milk, and white chocolate chips; peanut butter chips (if using); and walnuts. Drop by large spoonfuls onto the pans. Bake for about 10 minutes, or until the edges are nicely browned. Cool completely on wire racks.

BANANA CHOCOLATE CHIP SANDWICHES

Jennifer McCoy of Craft

Pastry chef McCoy rose to my challenge of making a cookie with bananas and chocolate chips. Her reinterpretation of the traditional chocolate chip cookie is quite wonderful. "We think they are a little more fun than the classic chocolate chip cookie," she says, "and we are now making them for the restaurant's petit four plate." · MAKES ABOUT 30 BITE-SIZE SANDWICH COOKIES

6 ounces (1½ sticks) unsalted butter, softened

¼ cup granulated sugar

¼ cup confectioners' sugar

½ teaspoon pure vanilla extract

1¾ cups all-purpose flour

¼ teaspoon salt

¾ cup mini semisweet chocolate chips

6 medium-ripe bananas

In the bowl of a stand mixer fitted with the paddle attachment, cream the butter, granulated sugar, confectioners' sugar, and vanilla on medium speed until light and fluffy. Reduce the speed to low and slowly add the flour and salt. Continue to mix until well incorporated. Slowly stir in the chocolate chips and continue to stir for about 1 minute.

Remove the dough from the mixer and place between 2 large sheets of parchment paper. Roll the dough to about ¼ inch thick. Remove the top layer of parchment, score the dough using a 1¼-inch round cookie cutter, and put the parchment back on top. Gently slide the sheet of dough onto a half-sheet pan and place in the freezer to chill for about 1 hour. (The dough can be prepared several days in advance.)

Preheat the oven to 325°F. Line three half-sheet pans with parchment paper.

Remove the dough from the freezer. Pop out the rounds of cut cookie dough. Arrange the rounds on the prepared pans, ½ inch apart. Bake for 8 to 10 minutes, or until light golden brown. Cool completely on wire racks.

Peel and cut the bananas into ½-inch-thick slices and sandwich each one between two chocolate chip cookies. Serve immediately.

CHOCOLATE CHIP EVERYTHING COOKIE
Robert Truitt of Corton

Chef Truitt and the pastry team at Corton make this sophisticated and diminutive treat often for the restaurant's family meal. It has become a cookie jar favorite in my house. · MAKES 90 TO 100 SMALL COOKIES

1 cup pecans

8 ounces (2 sticks) unsalted butter, softened

1 cup granulated sugar

1 cup packed dark brown sugar

1½ teaspoons kosher salt

2 large eggs

1 teaspoon pure vanilla extract

2½ cups bread flour

2½ tablespoons almond flour

1 teaspoon baking soda

1 cup old-fashioned rolled oats (not instant)

10 ounces (1⅔ cups) chopped dark or milk chocolate (or chocolate chips)

Preheat the oven to 375°F. Line a half-sheet pan with parchment paper.

Spread the pecans in a single layer on the prepared pan. Bake for 6 to 7 minutes, or until slightly browned and fragrant. Turn the oven off. Cool the pecans completely on the pan, then chop coarsely, and set aside.

In the bowl of a stand mixer fitted with the paddle attachment, cream the butter with the granulated sugar, brown sugar, and salt. Add the eggs, one at a time, scraping down the bowl between each addition. Add the vanilla.

Sift together the bread flour, almond flour, and baking soda, and fold into the butter mixture until just combined. Fold in the pecans, oats, and chocolate. Form the dough into a disk, wrap in plastic wrap and refrigerate overnight, or for at least 2 hours.

Preheat the oven to 375°F. Line four half-sheet pans with parchment paper.

Roll or scoop the dough into 1-inch balls. Arrange about 24 balls on each of the prepared pans. Bake for 7 to 9 minutes. Cool completely on wire racks.

CHOCOLATE CHIP COOKIES

Jacques Torres of Jacques Torres Chocolates

From the famed chocolatier, the recipe for this decadent cookie is not complicated. Chef Torres writes, "We feature these cookies all year long in our stores because they are so good, but I think they're best of all in the summer. We use them to make big, fat ice-cream sandwiches filled with our homemade vanilla, coffee, raspberry, strawberry, peanut butter, or chocolate ice cream. They are also a perennial picnic basket favorite. I don't think that I had ever eaten a chocolate chip cookie until I came to the States. But I sure have eaten my share since my arrival. Everybody seems to have a favorite recipe: some with nuts, some with added candies, and some with mixed chocolate pieces. This is my basic recipe." · MAKES ABOUT 36 LARGE COOKIES

4¾ cups all-purpose flour

2 teaspoons salt

1½ teaspoons baking powder

1½ teaspoons baking soda

12 ounces (3 sticks) unsalted butter, softened

2¼ cups packed light brown sugar

1¼ cups plus 2½ tablespoons granulated sugar

3 large eggs, at room temperature, lightly beaten

2 teaspoons pure vanilla extract

1⅔ pounds bittersweet chocolate, chopped into bite-size pieces

Preheat the oven to 325°F. Have ready four nonstick half-sheet pans, or line four regular half-sheet pans with parchment paper or silicone mats.

In a bowl, stir together the flour, salt, baking powder, and baking soda, and set aside.

In the bowl of a stand mixer fitted with the paddle attachment, beat the butter on medium speed for about 5 minutes, or until very light and fluffy. Add the brown sugar and granulated sugar, and beat until well blended. Add the eggs and beat just until incorporated. Beat in the vanilla. Reduce the speed to low and add the flour mixture a little at a time, beating after each addition until

incorporated. When all of the flour mixture has been incorporated, remove the bowl from the mixer and, using a silicone spatula, fold in the chocolate.

To shape the cookies, using a tablespoon, scoop out heaping spoonfuls of the dough and, using the palms of your hands, form them into 3-inch balls. Place the balls on the prepared pans, spacing them about 1 inch apart. Bake for about 15 minutes, or until lightly browned around the edges. Remove from the oven, transfer the cookies to wire racks, and let cool completely.

VARIATIONS

Apparently the original Toll House cookie was made much as I now make mine: by adding a cut-up chocolate bar to a butter-rich cookie dough. No need for any improvement! However, if you like, you can customize these cookies to make them your own: For chocolate chocolate chip cookies, replace 1 cup of the flour with Dutch-process cocoa powder. For a cake-like texture, replace 1 of the eggs with 2 egg yolks. For very moist cookies, replace 5½ tablespoons of the brown sugar and ½ cup of the granulated sugar with an equal amount of light corn syrup. And, of course, you can always add nuts (pecans, macadamias, or walnuts); raisins or other sweet dried fruits, such as cherries or cranberries; or candy bits.

CRAZY COWBOY COOKIES

Mario Batali and Benno Batali of Babbo

Chef Mario Batali created this recipe with his son, baker Benno. These cookies are sweet and salty, and fun to make. The kid in you will adore them. The Batalis confess, "Crazy cowboys love butterscotch and breakfast, and we love coconut, so we put these two together for our crazy cowboy friends—they seem to love them." · MAKES ABOUT 20 LARGE COOKIES

2 cups whole wheat flour

1½ teaspoons salt

1 teaspoon baking soda

1 teaspoon baking powder

8 ounces (2 sticks) unsalted butter, softened

½ cup granulated sugar

1 cup packed light brown sugar

2 large eggs

2 teaspoons pure almond extract

1½ cups old-fashioned rolled oats (not instant)

8 ounces (1⅓ cups) butterscotch chips

½ cup unsweetened shredded coconut

Preheat the oven to 350°F. Line three half-sheet pans with parchment paper.

Mix together the whole wheat flour, salt, baking soda, and baking powder in a medium bowl, and set aside.

In the bowl of a stand mixer fitted with the paddle attachment, beat the butter, granulated sugar, and brown sugar on medium-high speed until pale and creamy, about 3 minutes. Reduce the speed to medium. Add the eggs, one at a time, and beat well. Beat in the almond extract.

Reduce the speed to low, and slowly add the flour mixture, beating just until incorporated. Fold in the oats, butterscotch chips, and coconut until combined.

Using a soup spoon, drop the dough onto the prepared pans, spacing them 3 inches apart. Bake for 10 to 11 minutes, or until the edges of the cookies begin to brown. Remove from the oven and cool on top of the stove for 3 minutes, then transfer the cookies to wire racks. Let cool completely, but try one warm for quality control at this point . . . hey, you never know! (We store our cooled cookies in a snap-tight box with a heel of bread to keep them nice and chewy.)

PISTACHIO-CHERRY OATMEAL COOKIES

Daniel Humm of Eleven Madison Park

Chef Humm's favorite breakfast of granola with pistachios and cherries inspired these unusual oatmeal cookies. They are delightful and quite pretty. The sprinkling of sea salt is a subtle, sophisticated touch.

• MAKES ABOUT 70 SMALL COOKIES

13⅓ tablespoons unsalted butter, softened

1 cup granulated sugar

1¼ cups packed light brown sugar

1 teaspoon kosher salt

⅓ cup honey

2 teaspoons pure vanilla extract

½ cup extra virgin olive oil

3 large eggs

2⅔ cups bread flour

1½ cups old-fashioned rolled oats (not instant)

1½ teaspoons baking soda

3 cups pistachios, shelled

3 cups dried sour cherries

Fleur de sel, for sprinkling

In the bowl of a stand mixer fitted with the paddle attachment, cream the butter, granulated sugar, brown sugar, and salt. Mix in the honey, vanilla, and olive oil, and cream until light and fluffy. Add the eggs, one at a time; then add the flour, oats, and baking soda, and mix just until combined. With a silicone spatula, fold in the pistachios and dried cherries. Cover the bowl with plastic wrap, and refrigerate overnight.

Preheat the oven to 325°F. Line two half-sheet pans with parchment paper.

Using a small scoop, drop the dough onto the prepared pans, and lightly press down each cookie. Sprinkle with the fleur de sel. Bake for about 10 minutes, or until golden brown. Cool completely on wire racks.

CITY BAKERY OATMEAL RAISIN COOKIES

Maury Rubin of The City Bakery

When I asked baker Rubin (who taught me to bake tarts twenty years ago) for a recipe, I was thrilled that he shared this classic cookie with me. Popular with the City Bakery's loyal fans, they are oversized and never stay around my house long enough to get stale. · MAKES ABOUT 30 COOKIES

1½ cups organic all-purpose flour

1 teaspoon baking soda

2⅔ cups organic oats (such as Bob's Red Mill rolled organic oats)

8 ounces (2 sticks) unsalted butter, softened

¾ cup organic granulated sugar

1 cup plus 1 tablespoon organic packed light brown sugar

1 large egg

⅔ cup dark chocolate chips

⅓ cup raisins

Combine the flour, baking soda, and oats in a bowl and set aside.

In the bowl of a stand mixer fitted with the paddle attachment, cream the butter. Add the granulated sugar and brown sugar and mix, and then add the egg. Stop the machine and add half the flour mixture. When this mixture is incorporated, stop the machine again and repeat with the other half of the flour mixture. Fold in the chocolate chips and raisins just until combined. Remove the dough from the bowl, wrap in plastic wrap, and refrigerate for at least 6 hours, but 24 hours is best for the dough.

Preheat the oven to 350°F. Line two half-sheet pans with parchment paper.

Remove the dough from the refrigerator and let it soften at room temperature for about 20 minutes. Scoop out about 2 tablespoons of the dough for each cookie, and place on the prepared pans, spacing them 1 inch apart. Bake for 10 to 12 minutes, or until golden brown. Cool on wire racks for 15 minutes.

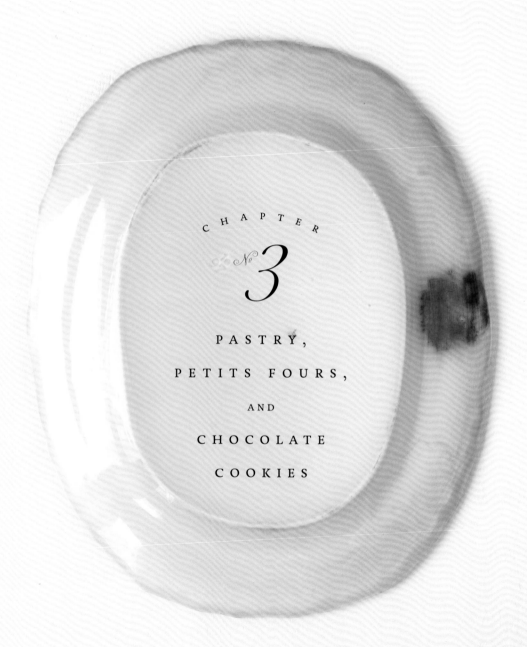

CHAPTER

№ 3

PASTRY,

PETITS FOURS,

AND

CHOCOLATE

COOKIES

QUENTIN'S GRANDMA'S RUGELACH

Jason Weiner and Risa Smith of Almond

A few years ago, Chef Weiner attended a baby shower in Brooklyn. There was a lot of delicious food at the party, but the showstopper was the transcendent rugelach. Never a fan of such pastries, he suddenly saw them in a new light. This recipe came from baby Quentin's grandmother, Risa Smith. She and the chef became fast friends, and the rest is history. Baker Risa now comes to the restaurant every Wednesday and knocks out rugelach for the week.

• MAKES ABOUT 36 RUGELACH

2¼ cups all-purpose flour

1 tablespoon granulated sugar

½ teaspoon fine sea salt

8 ounces (2 sticks) unsalted butter, cut into chunks and chilled

8 ounces cream cheese, cut into chunks

2 tablespoons sour cream or Greek yogurt

Pulse the flour, sugar, and salt in a food processor until combined. Add the butter and pulse until the mixture resembles coarse sand with some pea-size pieces of butter. Add the cream cheese and sour cream until the batter comes together into a rough dough. Turn the dough out of the bowl onto a floured work surface and divide into 4 portions. Pat each portion into a disk, wrap in plastic wrap, and chill in the refrigerator, about 45 minutes.

Meanwhile, make one of the following three fillings:

RAISIN FILLING

One 15-ounce box golden raisins

Enough water to cover the raisins

¼ cup granulated sugar

Pinch of salt

1 teaspoon ground cinnamon

1 teaspoon pure vanilla extract

½ cup walnuts (or filberts)

2 to 3 tablespoons rum

Put the raisins in a medium saucepan and cover with the water. Add the sugar, salt, cinnamon, and vanilla. Simmer over low heat until almost all the water is absorbed and the raisins are plumped. Transfer the raisin sauce to a blender or food processor and pulse. Add the walnuts and process again to form a paste. Add the rum to taste, and set aside to cool.

APRICOT FILLING

One 15-ounce box apricots

Enough water (or orange juice) to
   cover the apricots

¼ cup granulated sugar

Pinch of salt

1 teaspoon ground cinnamon

1 teaspoon pure vanilla extract

½ cup walnuts (or filberts)

One 12-ounce jar of orange
   marmalade

2 to 3 tablespoons orange brandy

Put the apricots in a medium saucepan and cover with the water. Add the sugar, salt, cinnamon, and vanilla. Simmer over low heat until almost all the water is absorbed and the apricots are soft and plumped. Transfer the apricot sauce to a blender or food processor and pulse. Add the walnuts and marmalade, and process again to form a paste. Add the brandy to taste, and set aside to cool.

CHOCOLATE FILLING

½ cup walnuts (or filberts)

8 ounces semisweet chocolate

¼ cup granulated sugar

1 teaspoon pure vanilla extract

1 tablespoon unsalted butter

One 12-ounce jar of seedless
   raspberry jam

2 to 3 tablespoons raspberry liqueur

Grind the walnuts until fine in a food processor, and set aside.

Place the chocolate in the top of a double boiler. Add the sugar, vanilla, and butter, and melt over low heat. Remove from the heat and stir in the jam and walnuts. Add the liqueur to taste, and set aside to cool.

2 large egg yolks   ¼ cup granulated sugar

Preheat the oven to 375°F. Line two half-sheet pans with parchment paper.

Roll 1 portion of the dough into a rectangle about ¼ inch thick. Spread on the filling. Starting with the long side, roll up the dough to make a tight cylinder. Flatten it a bit, and wrap in plastic wrap. Place the cylinder in the freezer or refrigerator, and continue this process with the remaining portions of dough.

Slice the cylinders into 1½-inch pieces, and place each piece seam side down on the prepared pans. Whisk the egg yolks and brush over the tops. Sprinkle with sugar. Bake about 25 minutes, or until golden and crispy. Cool for a few minutes on the pans. Transfer the rugelach to a wire rack to cool completely.

PALMIERS

Alain Sailhac of the French Culinary Institute

Chef Sailhac encouraged me to prepare the *feuilleté* (puff pastry) in the classic way for his crispy palmiers. Mastering the technique of creating the laminated dough from scratch is quite satisfying. However, if you don't have the time, purchase a good-quality frozen puff pastry instead. For this recipe, prepare your *mise en place* by measuring out all the ingredients at least four hours before baking.

• MAKES ABOUT 40 COOKIES

DÉTRAMPE

1 cup cake flour

1 cup all-purpose flour

1 teaspoon salt

3 tablespoons unsalted butter, softened

½ cup cold water

BEURRAGE

8 ounces (2 sticks) unsalted butter, chilled

Confectioners' sugar, for dusting

Granulated sugar, for dusting

Sift the cake flour, all-purpose flour, and salt onto a clean marble work surface. Make a well in the center and add the 3 tablespoons of softened butter. With your fingers, mix in the butter, slowly adding the cold water to form your dough. Pat the dough into a square shape. With a bench scraper, lift the dough, wrap it in plastic wrap, and place in the refrigerator for 30 minutes to rest. This is called the *détrampe*.

Now, prepare the *beurrage*. Place the 8 ounces chilled butter between 2 pieces of plastic wrap. Hit the package a few times with a rolling pin to slightly flatten and remove any lumps. Form the package into a square that is smaller than the *détrampe*, and place in the refrigerator for 25 minutes.

Dust the marble work surface with confectioners' sugar. Remove the *détrampe* from the refrigerator, and, keeping a square in the center about the same size as your *beurrage*, roll out four flaps, one on each side (north, south, east, and west). The flaps will be thinner than the center portion, and each should be large enough to fold over and cover most of the center.

Remove the *beurrage* from the refrigerator, and place in the center of the *détrampe*. Fold the flaps (north and south, then east and west) over the butter and seal the dough gently with your fingers. This is called the *pâton*.

Keeping the work surface dusted with confectioners' sugar, roll out the *pâton* into a long rectangle that is a little less than ¼ inch thick. Every time you roll, you should see the butter evenly spread under the top layer of dough. Fold the left side of the dough toward the center, then the right side. Roll out the dough again into a long rectangle. You have created two turns. Using your fingers, gently poke two indentations partway through the dough to indicate that you have made the two turns. Rewrap your *pâton* in plastic wrap and return it to the refrigerator.

After 1 hour, remove the *pâton* from the refrigerator, and make two more turns, dusting the surface with confectioners' sugar. Mark the dough with four finger indentations. Return the *pâton* to the refrigerator for 1 more hour; then repeat the process, dusting again with confectioners' sugar. You have now made six turns. The puff pastry is ready to turn into palmiers.

Preheat the oven to 400°F. Line two half-sheet pans with parchment paper.

Sprinkle granulated sugar on the work surface. Roll each of the long sides of the *pâton* toward the center, flattening them slightly. Then fold in half. Cut this cylinder into 1-inch-thick pieces, and place on the prepared pans, leaving space between each palmier.

Bake for 5 minutes, then turn the palmiers over and bake for another 5 minutes, until each side is a deep golden color. Cool completely on wire racks.

ANÍS BREDELE

Jean-Georges Vongerichten of Jean Georges

Chef Vongerichten fondly remembers his family's recipe for this special Alsatian Christmas cookie. "When I was a kid growing up in Alsace, my room was above the kitchen, and I could always smell what my mother and grandmother were cooking downstairs. At Christmastime, I would wake up to the wonderful smell of *anís* in the kitchen, and I knew my mother was making these cookies. I would run down to steal a few warm ones just out of the stove." Make these cookies tiny so that you can eat them by the handful without feeling guilty.

• MAKES 40 TO 50 SMALL COOKIES

2 large eggs

1 cup granulated sugar

One packet of vanilla sugar
  (such as Dr. Oetker brand)

1 tablespoon whole aniseeds

2 cups all-purpose flour, sifted, plus
  more for flouring the pan

Unsalted butter, for buttering the pan

Butter and flour a half-sheet pan.

In the bowl of a stand mixer fitted with the paddle attachment, beat the eggs with the sugar and vanilla sugar, until the mixture is thick and foamy and falls from the beater in a ribbon. Blend in the aniseeds and flour, and mix gently.

Using a piping bag with a plain 8-millimeter tip (such as Ateco #805), pipe out small mounds of batter about 1 inch in diameter onto the prepared pan. Let dry overnight in a cool, draft-free location.

Preheat the oven to 350°F.

Bake for 10 minutes. Cool completely on wire racks.

PETITS FOURS À L'ANISE

André Soltner of the French Culinary Institute

Fabled Lutèce restaurant host Chef Soltner told this charming story about his favorite childhood cookie. "I have seen these only in Alsace, nowhere else. When you bake them, they rise a little (and the tops spread) so they look like small mushrooms. These petits fours will keep for a long time in an airtight box. In Alsace every household has a box of *Anisbretle* always on hand to serve to unexpected visitors (with, of course, a glass of Alsatian white wine). But my grandmother had her own way of serving them. When we were children, my brother and I used to visit her every few weeks. She would serve us these cookies, and with them, even though we were small boys, a small glass of port."

• MAKES ABOUT 100 SMALL COOKIES

1 cup granulated sugar
3 large eggs
1 tablespoon whole aniseeds

2 cups all-purpose flour, sifted, plus
    more for flouring the pastry sheet
Unsalted butter, for buttering the
    pastry sheet

Butter a pastry sheet and dust it with flour.

Put the sugar and eggs in the bowl of an electric mixer. Mix for about 10 minutes at high speed, until a ribbon forms when a whisk is inserted and lifted from the mixture.

Add the aniseeds and beat for a few moments more, until the seeds are blended in.

By hand, with a spatula, gently fold in the flour. Put this dough in a pastry bag that is fitted with a round ½-inch tip.

Pipe the dough out of the pastry bag and onto the pastry sheet, forming circles about ¾ inch across. Let them dry overnight, or at least for 4 hours, at room temperature.

Preheat the oven to 275°F. Bake for about 10 minutes. Do not let the cookies brown. Cool completely on wire racks.

PETITS FOURS DE NOËL

André Soltner of the French Culinary Institute

Chef Soltner recalls the ritual of making these amazing Christmas cookies. "When I was young, every year, about three weeks before Christmas, all Alsatian housewives made these petits fours, which are called *Schwawebretle* in Alsatian. That was the beginning of the Christmas season and of the feelings of the Christmas spirit. Always, children helped their mothers to make the Christmas cookies. I did it when I was a child, and later my sister did it, and later my sister's children helped her. The little children climbed on the table where the dough was rolled out, and they stamped out the different shapes with cookie cutters." · MAKES ABOUT 100 SMALL COOKIES

8 ounces (2 sticks) unsalted butter, plus
   more for buttering the pastry sheet
1 cup granulated sugar
½ teaspoon powdered cinnamon
3 ounces commercial candied orange
   peel (optional)
8 ounces ground almonds

Grated zest of 1 lemon
3 small eggs
4 cups all-purpose flour, sifted, plus
   more for flouring the work surface
   and dusting the pastry sheet
1 small egg beaten with a little cold
   water

In a bowl, with a wooden spoon, work the butter until it is a soft paste. Add the sugar and work it in for a few minutes until smooth.

Add the cinnamon, candied orange peel (if using), almonds, lemon zest, and the 3 eggs, and mix thoroughly with a spatula. Add the flour and knead the mixture on a floured surface, or in the bowl, with your fingers, until you have a smooth paste.

Form the dough into a roll and enclose it in plastic wrap. Let this rest in the refrigerator overnight, or up to 2 to 3 days.

Preheat the oven to 300°F. Butter a pastry sheet and dust it with flour.

On a floured work surface, roll out the dough to a sheet ¼ inch thick. With cookie cutters, cut the dough into various shapes. Combine the remaining dough into a ball, and roll it out again on the floured work surface to a sheet ¼ inch thick. Cut again with cookie cutters. Repeat until all the dough is used up.

Arrange the cutouts on the pastry sheet. Brush them with the beaten egg. Bake in the preheated oven until they are golden brown—about 10 minutes. Cool completely on wire racks.

CHOCOLATE KNOBS

Isra Gordon of the French Culinary Institute

When you read the ingredients list for Chef Gordon's recipe, it appears to be one that would make a batch of classic cookies. However, chocolate knobs are actually more like old-fashioned chocolate candy.

• MAKES ABOUT 60 SMALL COOKIES

1 cup Dutch-process cocoa powder

⅛ teaspoon baking soda

¾ cup all-purpose flour

Pinch of salt

Pinch of ground cinnamon

4 ounces (1 stick) butter, softened

¾ cup granulated sugar

1 cup turbinado sugar

1 large egg, lightly beaten

¼ cup water

½ teaspoon pure vanilla extract

4 ounces dark chocolate chunks

4 ounces (½ cup) pecans, coarsely chopped

Preheat the oven to 350°F. Line two half-sheet pans with parchment paper.

Sift the cocoa powder, baking soda, flour, salt, and cinnamon into a medium bowl, and set aside.

In the bowl of a stand mixer fitted with the paddle attachment, cream the butter, granulated sugar, and turbinado sugar until well combined. Add the egg, water, and vanilla. Add the cocoa mixture. Fold in the chocolate and pecans.

Drop by rounded tablespoons onto the prepared pans. Bake for 10 to 12 minutes, or until slightly browned around the edges. Cool completely on wire racks.

FLOURLESS CHOCOLATE COOKIES

François Payard of François Payard Bakery

At Payard Patisserie, Chef Payard sold these cookies year-round, but they were especially popular during Passover because they contain no flour. About them he says, "Their crackled surfaces give them an elegant look, and because they are so easy and take barely any time to make, are great for last-minute entertaining. They have a slightly crunchy exterior, and a soft, almost brownie-like interior. They should be only about ½ inch at their thickest."

• MAKES ABOUT 12 COOKIES

½ cup plus 3 tablespoons Dutch-process cocoa powder

3 cups confectioners' sugar

Pinch of salt

2¾ cups walnuts, toasted and roughly chopped

4 large egg whites, at room temperature

1 tablespoon pure vanilla extract

Place a rack each in the upper and bottom thirds of the oven and preheat the oven to 350°F. Line two half-sheet pans with parchment paper or silicone baking mats.

Combine the cocoa powder, confectioners' sugar, salt, and walnuts in the bowl of an electric mixer fitted with the paddle attachment. Mix on low speed for 1 minute.

With the mixer running, slowly add the egg whites and vanilla. Mix on medium speed for 3 minutes, until the mixture has slightly thickened. Do not overmix it, or the egg whites will thicken too much.

With a 2-ounce cookie or ice-cream scoop, or a generous tablespoon, scoop the batter onto the prepared half-sheet pans, to make cookies that are 4 inches in diameter. Scoop 5 cookies onto each pan, about 3 inches apart so that they don't stick when they spread. If you have extra batter, wait until the first batch of cookies is baked before scooping the next batch.

Put the cookies in the oven, and immediately lower the temperature to 320°F. Bake for 14 to 16 minutes, or until small thin cracks appear on the surface of the cookies. Switch the pans halfway through baking. Pull the parchment paper with the cookies onto a wire cooling rack, and let cool completely before removing the cookies from the paper.

DOUBLE-CHOCOLATE FUDGE COOKIES
Amanda Moreno

When the first tray of pastry chef Moreno's soft, fudgy cookies came out of the oven, I sampled one immediately. It was so good that I had my husband hide the rest so that I wouldn't eat all of them before our family dinner. At dessert time, I found the cookies in the refrigerator in a bag he had labeled "liver," ensuring that no child of ours would ever touch them. I thought the cookies would be hard and ruined, but they were also quite good cold. • MAKES ABOUT 60 COOKIES

1 cup pistachios, shelled

12 ounces semisweet 66 percent chocolate

1½ ounces unsweetened 100 percent chocolate

8 ounces (2 sticks) butter, softened

½ cup granulated sugar

2 cups packed light brown sugar

½ teaspoon salt

6 large eggs

½ tablespoon pure vanilla extract

2 cups all-purpose flour

¾ teaspoon instant espresso powder

2¼ teaspoons baking powder

26 ounces semisweet or bittersweet chocolate chips

Preheat the oven to 325°F. Line three half-sheet pans with parchment paper.

Spread the pistachios in a single layer on one of the prepared pans. Roast gently, about 5 minutes. Cool completely on the pan. Set the parchment-lined pan aside. Grind the pistachios until fine in a food processor, and set aside.

Melt the semisweet chocolate and unsweetened chocolate in the top of a double boiler over medium heat. Set aside to cool.

In the bowl of a stand mixer fitted with the paddle attachment, cream the butter, granulated sugar, brown sugar, and salt. Add the eggs, one at a time, and vanilla. Pour in the cooled chocolate. Add the flour, espresso powder, and baking powder just until combined. Fold in the chocolate chips.

Drop the batter by rounded tablespoons onto the three prepared pans. Bake at 325°F for 6 minutes. Immediately after you remove the cookies from the oven, top them with the pistachio powder. Cool completely on wire racks.

PECAN AND CHOCOLATE COOKIES
Dominique Ansel of Daniel

Pastry chef Ansel mixes these wonderfully rich cookies the same way he would a batch of brownies. His technique is sheer brilliance. He recalls a visit to France. "It happened to be the birthdays of my niece and nephew. I had no time before-hand to buy a gift, so I pulled them into the kitchen. 'We're going to make these cookies together, and you get to pick what you want in them.' My niece chose the pecans, my nephew the chips. The cookies were perfect, and we didn't even care that they were lopsided."

• MAKES ABOUT 18 LARGE OR 36 SMALL COOKIES

11 ounces 66 percent chocolate (such as Valrhona Caraibe)
3 tablespoons unsalted butter
3 large eggs
1 cup plus 1 teaspoon granulated sugar
½ cup all-purpose flour
1 teaspoon baking powder
1 teaspoon salt
¾ cup 70 percent chocolate chips (such as Valrhona Guanaja) or 60 percent chocolate chips (such as Valrhona Caraibe) (optional)
½ cup pecan pieces (optional)

Preheat the oven to 325°F. Line two half-sheet pans with parchment paper.

In the top of a double boiler over low heat, melt the 66 percent chocolate and butter. Remove the mixture from the heat and set aside to cool for a few minutes.

In the bowl of a stand mixer fitted with the paddle attachment, beat the eggs and sugar. Add the chocolate mixture, then the flour, baking powder, and salt, and mix just until combined.

Remove the bowl from the mixer, and fold in the chocolate chips and pecans (if using).

Shape the batter into balls the size of golf balls, and arrange them on the prepared pans. Bake for 8 to 10 minutes, depending on the size of each cookie. The edges will feel done, but the centers will feel slightly underdone. Cool completely on wire racks.

ROMEO'S SIGHS AND JULIET'S KISSES
Tracey Zabar

In Verona, Italy, you can buy bags of *I baci di Romeo e Giulietta*—chocolate and almond cookies honoring Shakespeare's mythical, star-crossed lovers. I prefer to sandwich these two types of cookies together by sealing the "sighs" and "kisses" with a sweet filling. You will need two sets of mixer bowls and paddle attachments for this recipe. • MAKES ABOUT 30 SANDWICH COOKIES

ROMEO'S SIGHS

4 ounces (1 stick) unsalted butter, softened

½ cup granulated sugar

½ teaspoon pure almond extract

½ teaspoon salt

1 cup all-purpose flour, sifted

Preheat the oven to 350°F. Line two half-sheet pans with parchment paper.

In the bowl of a stand mixer fitted with the paddle attachment, cream the butter and sugar. Add the almond extract. Add the salt and flour, beating just until each addition is incorporated.

Drop by rounded teaspoonfuls onto one of the prepared pans. Set aside until you prepare Juliet's Kisses.

JULIET'S KISSES

4 ounces (1 stick) unsalted butter, softened

½ cup granulated sugar

1 teaspoon pure vanilla extract

½ teaspoon salt

¾ cup all-purpose flour, sifted

¼ cup Dutch-process cocoa powder, sifted

In the bowl of a stand mixer fitted with the paddle attachment, cream the butter and sugar. Add the vanilla. Add the salt, flour, and cocoa powder, beating just until each addition is incorporated.

Drop by level teaspoonfuls onto the second prepared pan. (These cookies spread more than the Romeos.)

Place the pan of Romeos and the pan of Juliets in the center of the oven. Bake 8 to 10 minutes, or until the Romeos just start to brown at the edges. Cool completely on wire racks.

FILLING
1 cup Nutella, raspberry jam, or
   melted bittersweet chocolate

Spread the filling onto the flat side of a Romeo and sandwich together with a Juliet. Repeat this process with the remaining cookies.

CHAPTER

№ *4*

MERINGUES,

MACARONS,

AND

MACAROONS

PINK SWIRL AND DUSTED MERINGUES

Tracey Zabar

These meringues, a favorite of Stanley and Saul Zabar of Zabar's, are often called clouds due to their appearance. They are also known as nighty-nights or forgotten cookies because you can put them in the oven, shut off the gas, and forget about them until morning. Avoid making the meringues on rainy or humid days, as they will be sticky. · MAKES ABOUT 45 COOKIES

2 large egg whites
½ teaspoon pure vanilla extract
¼ teaspoon salt

⅓ cup granulated sugar
1 drop pink or red food coloring
Decorative sugar, for dusting

Preheat the oven to 350°F. Line two half-sheet pans with parchment paper.

In the bowl of a stand mixer fitted with the whip attachment, beat the egg whites until foamy. (Make sure that you use a metal bowl, and that it, the whip, and spatula are perfectly clean and dry. One spot of grease will prevent the egg whites from reaching stiff peaks.)

Add the vanilla and salt and continue beating. Add the sugar slowly, 1 tablespoon at a time, until the mixture is shiny, and stiff peaks have formed.

Add color to the cookies by putting 1 drop of food coloring on the inside of a piping bag, fitted with a decorative tip (such as Ateco #824). Gently fill the bag with the meringue mixture. Pipe the cookies onto the prepared pans. Dust with decorative sugar. Place them in the oven, and immediately turn off the heat. Leave the pans in the oven, without opening the door, for at least 6 hours, or overnight.

NOTE: Do not make the meringues in a convection oven, because when you turn off the oven, a cooling fan turns on and the cookies will not dry out.

GRANDMA TROWER'S CORNFLAKE MERINGUES

My great friend Alex's grandmother made similar meringues, except that she gently added ½ cup cornflakes after the mixture formed stiff peaks.

BRUTTI MA BUONI
Cesare Casella of Salumeria Rosi

Brutti ma buoni translates to "ugly but tasty." Despite their appearance, these meringues are indeed delicious. "The recipe," Chef Casella writes, "was imported to Tuscany from Piedmont, when Florence briefly reigned as Italy's capital. In Prato, they're considered the sister sweet to the famous *cantucci* (anise-scented almond biscotti). I love their light crunchiness. Pack a box of these cookies and a bottle of Chardonnay for a perfect picnic ending."

• MAKES ABOUT 100 COOKIES

5 cups blanched almonds, divided
1½ cups granulated sugar
¼ teaspoon ground cinnamon

½ cup candied fruit, finely chopped
  (optional)
Pinch of salt
7 large egg whites

Preheat the oven to 325°F. Butter two half-sheet pans.

Place the almonds on a half-sheet pan and toast until lightly colored, about 8 to 10 minutes.

In a food processor, coarsely chop 2½ cups of the toasted almonds and transfer them to a bowl. Finely grind the remaining almonds, then add them to the coarsely chopped almonds, along with the sugar, cinnamon, and candied fruit (if using). Set aside.

Add a pinch of salt to the egg whites and using an electric mixer fitted with the whip attachment, on the second highest speed, beat to medium peaks. Fold a third of the egg whites at a time into the almond mixture.

Drop the batter by teaspoonfuls, about 1½ inches apart, onto the prepared pans. Bake until the cookies are golden brown, 15 to 20 minutes. Cool completely on wire racks.

The cookies will keep in an airtight container for 1 to 2 weeks.

NONNY'S MINT CHOCOLATE CHIP MERINGUE COOKIES

Richard Grausman of Careers Through Culinary Arts Program (C-CAP)

If you crave mints, you will savor these pretty confections. About their origin, Richard Grausman explains, "My late mother-in-law, Selma Pearl, was known to her friends and dinner guests for her stylish parties and beautiful presentations. But to our daughters, 'Nonny' was famous for her bedtime treats. None were more loved and constantly requested than her 'green cookies.' I hope that everyone who tries this easy-to-make treat will love them too."

• MAKES ABOUT 45 COOKIES

12 ounces (2 cups) semisweet
   chocolate chips
1¼ teaspoons pure peppermint
   extract, divided

2 large egg whites
⅓ cup plus 1 tablespoon granulated
   sugar
4 drops green food coloring

Combine the chocolate chips and 1 teaspoon of the peppermint extract in a resealable plastic bag. Turn the bag several times to ensure coating. Place in the refrigerator for 12 to 24 hours.

Preheat the oven to 200°F. Line two half-sheet pans with Silpats (nonstick baking mats) or parchment paper.

In a medium bowl, beat the egg whites until soft peaks form, and then beat in the sugar until stiff. Add the food coloring and the remaining ¼ teaspoon peppermint extract, and beat until combined. With a silicone spatula, fold in the chocolate chips.

Drop by rounded teaspoons onto the prepared pans, spacing them close together—they will not spread. Bake for 1 hour, then turn off the heat and allow the meringues to cool in the oven for several hours or overnight.

Remove the cookies from the half-sheet pans and store them in a tightly covered container.

RASPBERRY FRENCH *MACARONS*

Florian Bellanger and Ludovic Augendre of Mad Mac

Master pastry chefs Bellanger and Augendre (who met while baking at the legendary Parisian gourmet store Fauchon) make some of the best *macarons* I have ever tasted. These impossibly fragile and pretty cookies are not as difficult to make as they look. Take a deep breath and follow the instructions.

• MAKES ABOUT 24 *MACARONS*

1 cup almond flour

⅓ cup plus 1 tablespoon confectioners' sugar

2 large egg whites, divided

1 tablespoon apricot jam

⅓ cup granulated sugar

Pink or red food coloring, as needed

One 12-ounce jar raspberry preserves with seeds (preferably Bonne Maman)

Preheat the oven to 375°F. Line two half-sheet pans with parchment paper.

Using a whisk, combine the almond flour and confectioners' sugar in a bowl. Add 1 egg white and the apricot jam, and mix until combined. Set aside.

In the bowl of a stand mixer fitted with the whip attachment, beat the remaining egg white until foamy. Add the granulated sugar gradually, 1 tablespoon at a time, until stiff peaks form. Add enough food coloring to this meringue to make a nice, bright pink—the color will fade a bit during baking.

With a silicone spatula, gently fold one-third of the meringue into the almond flour mixture. Repeat with the next third of the meringue, and combine. Repeat with the last third of the meringue, and mix until combined and shiny.

Using a piping bag with a large plain tip (such as Ateco #804), form 1-inch-diameter *macaron* shells on the prepared pans. Let the shells rest at room temperature for about 15 minutes, or until the tops have dried out. You can test that they are sufficiently dried out if the batter does not stick to your fingertip.

Bake the shells for 12 to 14 minutes. Cool completely on the pans. They will be very fragile. Gently lift the shells from the parchment-lined pans, and flip them over. Using your thumb, press the center to make a small indentation in each shell. With a teaspoon or a piping bag fitted with a plain tip, pipe dollops of the raspberry preserves into the indented sides of half the shells. Sandwich them together with the remaining shells.

Refrigerate the *macarons* overnight on a tray covered with plastic wrap or in an airtight container. They will absorb some moisture from the preserves and become more tender.

PISTACHIO COOKIES

Fortunato Nicotra of Felidia

Reminiscent of the traditional Sicilian almond cookie called *maccarone*, this lovely green treat is very simple to prepare. With the added pistachio flavor, Chef Nicotra's version is the ultimate Christmas cookie.

• MAKES ABOUT 200 MINIATURE COOKIES OR 60 LARGE COOKIES

1 pound almond paste

1½ tablespoons pistachio paste

½ cup granulated sugar

2 to 3 large egg whites

Preheat the oven to 350°F. Line two half-sheet pans with parchment paper.

In a stand mixer fitted with the paddle attachment, mix the almond paste, pistachio paste, and sugar together until smooth. Slowly add in the egg whites and continue to mix until fully incorporated.

To make miniature cookies, fill a disposable pastry bag with the cookie mixture, and cut a small tip off the bottom of the bag. With the tip about ¼ inch from the surface of the prepared pan, pipe the mixture into cookies that are the size of Hershey's Kisses. Bake the cookies for 7 to 9 minutes. Halfway through baking, reverse the pans in the oven, so the cookies bake evenly. Remove the pans, and let the cookies cool on wire racks for about 5 minutes.

To make large cookies, fill a disposable pastry bag with the cookie mixture, and cut off the tip slightly smaller than the size round you would like. With the tip about ½ inch from the surface of the prepared pan, pipe the mixture into rounds about 2 inches in diameter. Bake the cookies for 10 to 12 minutes. Halfway through baking, reverse the pans in the oven, so the cookies bake evenly. Remove the pans, and let the cookies cool on wire racks for about 5 minutes.

JAM-TOPPED PISTACHIO COOKIES

To dress up these cookies, once you have piped the mixture onto the half-sheet pan, fill each morsel with fresh preserves or jam: Wet your thumb and gently push down the center of each cookie—creating a little thumbprint. Bake the cookies for the recommended times given and allow them to cool completely on wire racks before filling each little nook.

COCONUT-NUTELLA-ALMOND MACAROONS

Pichet Ong of Spot Dessert Bar

Chef Ong's beautiful and delicious cookies are quite large. They make a great alternative to the ubiquitous birthday cupcake, and are far more sophisticated.

• MAKES ABOUT 12 MACAROONS

¼ cup slivered almonds

2 large egg whites

½ cup granulated sugar

⅛ teaspoon table salt

½ teaspoon pure vanilla extract

1½ cups unsweetened shredded coconut

⅓ cup Nutella

Maldon sea salt, for sprinkling

Preheat the oven to 325°F. Line a half-sheet pan with parchment paper.

Spread the almonds in a single layer on the prepared pan. Bake until toasted, about 6 to 8 minutes. Cool completely, transfer to a medium bowl, and set aside. Set the prepared pan aside for baking the macaroons. Keep the oven on.

In the bowl of a stand mixer fitted with the whisk attachment, whip the egg whites with the sugar and table salt until frothy. Whisk in the vanilla until well combined. Fold in the coconut.

With a silicone or offset spatula, spread the batter onto the prepared pan and place another piece of parchment on top. With a rolling pin, roll the covered batter until it is even. Remove the top piece of parchment.

Bake for 10 to 12 minutes, or until the top is toasted and dry to the touch. Remove from the oven and while the macaroon is still warm, cut it into 12 rectangular pieces. Cool completely on wire racks.

Spread Nutella on the top of each cookie, then spread the toasted almonds over it. Sprinkle with a small amount of Maldon sea salt.

COCONUT MACAROONS

Sarabeth Levine of Sarabeth's Bakery

Sarabeth's Bakery sells these flourless treats during Passover, but they are excellent all year long. Not your ordinary store-bought macaroons, master baker Sarabeth Levine's cookies are plump, chewy, and very moist because the mixture absorbs the sugary syrup. For the best flavor, use unsweetened shredded coconut, available at natural food stores, rather than sweetened coconut flakes.

• MAKES ABOUT 24 MACAROONS

1½ cups granulated sugar

⅓ cup water

2 teaspoons light corn syrup

Pinch of fine sea salt

½ teaspoon pure vanilla extract

Grated zest of ½ orange

5 cups (1 pound) unsweetened
   shredded coconut

3 large egg whites, at room
   temperature

Position a rack in the center of the oven and preheat the oven to 325°F. Line a half-sheet pan with parchment paper.

Combine the sugar, water, corn syrup, and salt in a heavy-bottomed medium saucepan. Bring to a boil over high heat, stirring just until the sugar dissolves. Pour into the bowl of a stand mixer. Add the vanilla and orange zest, and stir with a silicone spatula to combine.

Attach the bowl to the mixer and affix the paddle attachment. With the mixer on low speed, gradually add the coconut. Then, gradually pour in the egg whites and mix into a dough. Let stand for 10 minutes.

Using a 1½-inch-diameter ice-cream scoop, scoop up the coconut mixture. With your other hand, lightly compress the mixture into the scoop so it will hold its shape better when released onto the pan. Release the coconut mixture onto the prepared pan. Repeat with the remaining mixture, spacing the mounds about 1 inch apart. Bake for about 20 minutes, or until the macaroons are light golden brown. Cool completely on the pan.

The cookies can be stored in an airtight container at room temperature for 5 days.

RASPBERRY COCONUT MACAROONS
Gently fold in 1 cup frozen crumbled raspberries to the completed dough and bake as directed.

CHOCOLATE-DRIZZLED COCONUT MACAROONS
After the macaroons have been baked and cooled, drizzle them with tempered chocolate for an added treat.

TRIBECA GRILL'S COCONUT MACAROONS

Stéphane Motir of Tribeca Grill

Chef Motir's coconut macaroons, which have been a part of the restaurant's signature cookie plate for years, are very simple to make. You can whip up a batch of these sweets in no time. · MAKES ABOUT 75 MACAROONS

1 pound sweetened coconut flakes
1 teaspoon pure vanilla extract
Pinch of salt

⅔ cup sweetened condensed milk
2 large egg whites

Preheat the oven to 375°F. Line two half-sheet pans with parchment paper.

Combine the coconut flakes, vanilla, salt, and condensed milk in a bowl, and set aside.

In the bowl of a stand mixer fitted with the whip attachment, beat the egg whites until stiff. With a silicone spatula, gently fold the egg whites into the coconut mixture.

Shape the mixture into 1-inch balls and place on the prepared pans. Bake for 7 to 10 minutes, or until golden brown. Cool completely on wire racks.

CHOCOLATE-DIPPED MACAROONS

Dip the cooled macaroons halfway into a bowl of tempered bittersweet or semisweet chocolate. Place them on a parchment-lined half-sheet pan until the chocolate hardens.

BISCOTTI,

SPICE COOKIES,

AND

SEED COOKIES

CINNAMON-SCENTED FIG AND WALNUT BISCOTTI

Micol Negrin of Rustico Cooking

Chef Negrin and her husband, Dino De Angelis, run an extraordinary cooking school in New York. Every time I bake with them, I feel as if I am in Italy. She says, "These biscotti highlight the complex sweetness of dried figs, a specialty of Calabria, where they grow plump and sweet under intense sun and are then transformed into countless simple yet satisfying desserts. I developed the recipe after a trip to Calabria, when I was craving the flavors of the fig-laced, cinnamon-scented sweets we sampled there. For best results, use good-quality, juicy figs, not overly dried ones. If the figs are hard to chop, toss them with a little of the flour from the measured ingredients so they don't stick together."

• MAKES ABOUT 48 COOKIES

1 cup shelled walnut halves

8 dried figs, finely chopped (¾ cup)

1½ cups unbleached all-purpose flour (scooped, not spooned)

1 cup granulated sugar, plus extra for the counter

¼ teaspoon ground cinnamon

Grated zest of 1 large orange

1 envelope Italian baking powder (such as Lievito Pane Degli Angeli) or 1 teaspoon baking powder

⅛ teaspoon sea salt

2 large eggs

1½ teaspoons pure vanilla extract

Preheat the oven to 350°F (preferably set on convection bake). Line two half-sheet pans with parchment paper.

Coarsely chop the walnuts in a food processor. Do not over-process them; they should be the size of large peas. (If they are ground rather than chopped, the batter will be too dry and will require additional eggs to come together.) Turn the walnuts out into a large bowl. Add the figs, flour, sugar, cinnamon, orange zest, baking powder, and salt, and mix well to combine.

In a small bowl, beat the eggs with the vanilla. Pour the egg mixture into the flour mixture and stir with a fork until the dough just starts to come together.

Gather the dough with your hands, squeezing and kneading it firmly to help it form a solid mass.

Turn the dough out onto a counter, gather into a tight ball, and cut into 4 equal pieces. (If the dough sticks to the counter, sprinkle the counter with a bit of sugar, not flour.) Shape each piece into a 1-inch-wide log, and place the logs, 2 inches apart, on the prepared pans. Bake for 25 minutes, or until lightly golden and just set. Remove to a cutting board, cool for 5 minutes, and cut on the diagonal into ¼-inch-thick slices.

Arrange the slices in a single layer on the same parchment-lined pans. Return to the oven and bake for 8 minutes, or until golden; the biscotti will not be fully crisp. Cool on a rack, and serve.

WICKED CHOCOLATE BISCOTTI

Tracey Zabar

When I decided to make chocolate biscotti, I reviewed my collection of recipes and noticed that they were very similar, except that one called for instant coffee, another for grated orange zest. Others had a lot of vanilla, chips, and nuts. For some, olive oil was substituted for butter. For my version, I went with butter and combined generous quantities of the ingredients from each recipe. The result is delicious biscotti that are not too dry. • MAKES ABOUT 45 COOKIES

1 cup pistachios, shelled (or pecans
   or hazelnuts)
4 ounces (1 stick) butter, softened
1 cup granulated sugar
2 large eggs
2 teaspoons pure vanilla extract
Grated zest of 1 orange
½ cup Dutch-process cocoa powder,
   sifted

2 teaspoons instant espresso powder
2 teaspoons baking powder
½ teaspoon salt
2 cups all-purpose flour
6 ounces (1 cup) semisweet chocolate
   chips
½ cup sanding (coarse) sugar

Preheat the oven to 350°F. Line two half-sheet pans with parchment paper.

Spread the pistachios in a single layer on one of the prepared pans. Bake for 6 to 8 minutes, or until the nuts are lightly browned and fragrant. Cool completely on the pan. Transfer the nuts to a bowl, and set aside the prepared pan to reuse to bake the biscotti.

In the bowl of a stand mixer fitted with the paddle attachment, cream the butter and granulated sugar. Add the eggs, vanilla, and orange zest. Add the cocoa powder, espresso powder, baking powder, salt, and flour, and mix just until combined. With a wooden spoon, fold in the pistachios and chocolate chips.

Sprinkle the sanding sugar on the parchment in each prepared pan. Divide the dough into 4 pieces. Roll out each piece into a log, about 12 inches long and 2 inches in diameter. The dough will be somewhat sticky. Place 2 logs on each of the pans and roll them in the sanding sugar until most of it coats.

Bake for 25 to 30 minutes, making sure the logs do not start to burn. Remove the logs from the oven, and leave the oven turned on. Cool for about 10 minutes, then cut the logs diagonally into 1-inch pieces. (It is perfectly acceptable if the logs have some cracks on the top or crumble a bit under the knife blade.) Lay the cookies flat side down on the pans and return the pans to the oven for 5 minutes. Remove from the oven, flip the cookies over, and return to the oven for another 5 minutes to dry out. Cool completely on wire racks.

CHOCOLATE BISCUITS

For softer cookies, remove the logs from the oven, and cool about 10 minutes. Cut diagonally into 1-inch pieces, and cool completely on wire racks. Baked only once, these cookies are not technically biscotti (which means "twice baked").

BISCOTTI ALLE MANDORLE

Anna Teresa Callen of the James Beard Foundation

Some biscotti recipes contain butter, while others call for olive oil. This delightful version has both. "These classic almond biscotti are made everywhere in Italy," Chef Callen writes. "My grandmother, Nonnina, as we affectionately called her, used to make them all the time. She would always have them ready for visitors. The beverages varied depending on the person to whom the cookies were served. Tea or hot chocolate for the ladies; for others, the special wine *vino cotto*, perfect for dipping." For this recipe, you can use hazelnuts, peanuts, or walnuts instead of almonds. • MAKES ABOUT 24 COOKIES

6 ounces (1½ sticks) unsalted butter, divided

3 cups all-purpose flour, plus ½ cup for kneading

2 teaspoons baking powder

4 large eggs

1 cup granulated sugar

3 tablespoons olive oil

1 teaspoon pure almond extract

1 teaspoon pure vanilla extract

1 cup skinned almonds, lightly toasted and coarsely chopped

Preheat the oven to 350°F. Line a baking pan with parchment or waxed paper and brush lightly with ½ stick melted butter.

Sift the flour and baking powder together. Set aside. Melt 1 stick of butter and set aside.

In the bowl of a stand mixer fitted with the paddle attachment, combine the eggs and sugar. Beat for 5 minutes, then add 1 stick melted butter. Mix briefly and add the olive oil, almond extract, vanilla, and chopped almonds. Gradually add the flour mixture and beat until well combined.

Transfer the dough to a floured board and knead for 5 to 8 minutes, adding more flour if necessary. Shape the dough into two 14 by 2-inch loaves. Place on the prepared pan. Bake until golden, about 25 minutes. Cool on a rack.

Reduce the oven temperature to 275°F.

Cut the loaves diagonally with a serrated knife into 1-inch slices. Return the slices to the pan and bake for 10 minutes. Turn the cookies over, and continue baking for 10 more minutes. Cool completely on wire racks before storing the cookies in airtight containers.

GINGER CITRUS COOKIES

Marcus Samuelsson of Red Rooster

"The smell of gingersnaps always reminds me of my childhood in Sweden," recalls Chef Samuelsson. "We traditionally eat these cookies, called *pepparkakor*, at Christmas, though now they're eaten year-round. I add candied citrus to mine for a pop of tangy sweetness that tastes perfect against the spicy ginger. The holiday season is a magical time of year in Sweden, and one bite of these cookies transports me back home in an instant." To make the spices fragrant and intense, toast them in a saucepan at the start. You can substitute store-bought high-quality candied citrus peel for the homemade. Avoid supermarket candied peel; good candied orange peel is available at gourmet markets and by mail order.

• MAKES ABOUT 60 COOKIES

1 teaspoon ground ginger

¼ teaspoon ground cloves

½ teaspoon ground cinnamon

½ teaspoon ground cardamom

3½ cups sifted all-purpose flour

1 tablespoon baking soda

1 teaspoon salt

½ teaspoon freshly ground white
  pepper

5 ounces (1¼ sticks) unsalted butter,
  softened

1 cup granulated sugar

½ cup packed light brown sugar

2 large eggs

¾ cup molasses

1 cup finely chopped Candied Citrus
  Peel (recipe follows)

Preheat the oven to 350°F. Line two half-sheet pans with parchment paper.

Toast the ginger, cloves, cinnamon, and cardamom in a small skillet over medium heat, stirring with a wooden spoon, for 2 to 3 minutes, until fragrant. Remove from the heat.

Sift the flour, toasted spices, baking soda, salt, and white pepper into a bowl or onto a sheet of waxed paper.

In a large bowl, beat the butter, granulated sugar, and brown sugar with an electric mixer until light and fluffy. Add the eggs, one at a time, beating well after each addition and scraping down the sides of the bowl as necessary. Beat in the molasses. Gradually fold in the flour mixture. Stir in the candied citrus peel.

To make perfectly shaped cookies that are all the same size, use a small (#30) ice-cream scoop to drop the dough onto the prepared pans, spacing the cookies 2 inches apart. Bake for 10 to 12 minutes, until the tops feel firm when lightly touched. Cool on the half-sheet pans for about 2 minutes, then transfer the cookies to a wire rack to cool completely.

Stored in an airtight container, the cookies will keep for up to 1 month.

CANDIED CITRUS PEEL • MAKES ABOUT 1 CUP

2 cups strips or slices of lemon, lime, orange, and/or grapefruit peel (remove the peel with a sharp knife, then slice off the innermost bitter white pith, leaving a ¼-inch-thick layer)

2 cups water, plus extra for boiling the peel
2 cups granulated sugar, plus extra for coating (optional)

Put the citrus peel in a medium saucepan, cover with plenty of cold water, and bring to a boil; drain. Repeat two more times.

Combine the 2 cups water and sugar in a medium saucepan and bring to a boil, stirring to dissolve the sugar. Add the citrus peel and bring just to a simmer, then reduce the heat to low and simmer very gently for 30 to 45 minutes, until the peel is translucent. Remove from the heat and let the peel cool in the syrup.

If you are using the candied peel for the ginger citrus cookies, drain and finely chop. If you want to sugarcoat the candied peel on its own, drain well, spread a layer of sugar on a plate, and toss the citrus peel, in batches, in the sugar. Transfer to wire racks to dry.

GINGERSNAPS

William Gallagher of Becco

As they bake, these flavor-packed cookies puff up like dreamy little pillows. Chef Gallagher's unusual method of chilling, then cutting and freezing, makes this dough simple to handle. · MAKES ABOUT 75 COOKIES

4 cups all-purpose flour

1 tablespoon baking soda

⅔ teaspoon salt

1 tablespoon ground cinnamon

2½ teaspoons ground ginger

Pinch of freshly ground black pepper

11 ounces (2¾ sticks) unsalted butter, softened

1¾ cups granulated sugar

⅔ teaspoon pure vanilla extract

2 large eggs

½ cup molasses

½ cup turbinado sugar, as needed

Line a half-sheet pan with plastic wrap, leaving enough overhang to completely cover the dough.

Sift together the flour, baking soda, salt, cinnamon, ginger, and pepper into a large bowl, and set aside.

In the bowl of a stand mixer fitted with the paddle attachment, cream the butter and sugar, scraping the sides as necessary. Add the vanilla and eggs, and cream again. Add the molasses, and mix well. Add the flour mixture, scraping the sides of the bowl to ensure that there are no butter streaks in the dough. Pack the dough into the plastic-lined pan, and cover with the overhang. Chill thoroughly. Cut into two-inch-wide bars. Rewrap in plastic wrap, and freeze.

Preheat the oven to 350°F. Line three half-sheet pans with parchment paper.

Slice the bars into ¼-inch slices, dip one side of each in turbinado sugar, and place on the prepared pans. Bake for 8 to 10 minutes, or just until the edges start to brown. Cool completely on wire racks.

GINGERSNAP COOKIES
Michael Laiskonis of Le Bernardin

Chef Laiskonis described these spicy and fragrant gingersnaps to me. "I love these cookies, not just for their complex flavor, but also because the texture can vary according to whim—soft and chewy, or crisp and crunchy," he said. "The gingersnap also makes a great sandwich cookie; fill with a citrusy buttercream or even ice cream." For ease in slicing the crystallized ginger, sprinkle it first with granulated sugar, and be sure to use a sharp knife. · MAKES ABOUT 48 COOKIES

2 cups all-purpose flour

2 teaspoons baking powder

1 teaspoon ground ginger

¼ teaspoon ground cinnamon

¼ teaspoon ground cloves

¼ teaspoon ground cardamom

5 tablespoons plus 2 teaspoons
  unsalted butter, softened

1 cup plus 2 tablespoons granulated
  sugar

1 large egg

2 teaspoons white vinegar

½ cup molasses

2 tablespoons finely chopped
  crystallized ginger

Sift together the flour, baking powder, ground ginger, cinnamon, cloves, and cardamom, and set aside.

In the bowl of a stand mixer fitted with the paddle attachment, combine the butter and sugar, and cream until light and fluffy. Add the egg, vinegar, and molasses, then the chopped crystallized ginger. Add the flour mixture, and beat just until combined. Cover the bowl with plastic wrap and refrigerate or freeze.

Preheat the oven (preferably set on convection) to 325°F. Line two half-sheet pans with parchment paper.

Drop tablespoon-size balls of dough onto the prepared pans, allowing ample space for spreading. Lightly flatten each ball of dough. For chewier cookies, bake for 10 minutes, or until browned around the edges. For a crispier cookie, bake an additional 5 minutes, or until the color becomes a uniform brown. Let the cookies cool completely on wire racks before serving.

GINGERBREAD PEOPLE

Waldy Malouf of Beacon

Chef Malouf enjoys making these spicy mini gingerbread people at Christmas-time. He explains, "About twenty years ago, after I made gingerbread houses with my daughter at the Hudson River Club, she developed an insatiable taste for gingerbread. So we created these cookies for her. She also enjoyed deco-rating, or more accurately *"shmearing,"* them with royal icing. They are now a family tradition during the holidays." · MAKES ABOUT 60 SMALL COOKIES

3 cups all-purpose flour

3 tablespoons ground ginger

1 tablespoon ground cinnamon

¼ cup water

1¼ teaspoons baking soda

1 cup molasses

8 ounces (2 sticks) unsalted butter, softened

¾ cup packed light brown sugar

1 teaspoon salt

1 teaspoon finely grated fresh ginger

Sift together the flour, ground ginger, and cinnamon into a large bowl, and set aside. In a medium bowl, combine the water, baking soda, and molasses, and set aside.

In the bowl of a stand mixer fitted with the paddle attachment, cream the butter and brown sugar until light and fluffy. Mix in the salt and fresh ginger. Add the flour mixture alternately with the molasses mixture and mix until combined. Cover the bowl with plastic wrap, and chill the dough in the refrig-erator for 3 to 4 hours or overnight.

Preheat the oven to 350°F. Line two half-sheet pans with parchment paper.

On a lightly floured surface, roll out the dough to ⅛ inch thick, and cut into shapes with cookie cutters. Transfer the cookies to the prepared pans. Bake for 7 to 10 minutes, or until lightly browned on the edges. Cool on wire racks.

1 pound confectioners' sugar

⅛ teaspoon cream of tartar

3 large egg whites (or pasteurized
egg whites)

In the bowl of a stand mixer fitted with the whisk attachment, whip the confectioners' sugar, cream of tartar, and egg whites together until light and fluffy.

Pipe the icing (if using) onto the cookies, or spread with an offset spatula.

SUGAR-TOPPED MOLASSES SPICE COOKIES

Laurent Tourondel of Brasserie Ruhlmann

Chef Tourondel's spicy, chewy cookies are perfect holiday gifts because they are great candidates for shipping. Stack the cookies one on top of another between squares of parchment or waxed paper. · MAKES ABOUT 24 COOKIES

2⅓ cups all-purpose flour
2 teaspoons baking soda
½ teaspoon salt
½ teaspoon ground cinnamon
2 teaspoons ground ginger
¼ teaspoon ground allspice
Pinch of freshly ground black pepper

6 ounces (1½ sticks) unsalted butter,
   softened
1 cup packed light brown sugar
½ cup molasses
1 large egg
½ cup granulated sugar for rolling

Whisk together the flour, baking soda, salt, cinnamon, ginger, allspice, and pepper in a large bowl, and set aside.

In the bowl of a stand mixer fitted with the paddle attachment, beat the butter until smooth and creamy. Add the brown sugar and molasses and beat for 2 minutes. Add the egg and beat for an additional 1 minute. Reduce the speed to low. Carefully add the flour mixture gradually, and mix until well combined. Divide the dough in half, and wrap each piece in plastic wrap. Freeze for 30 minutes.

Preheat the oven to 350°F. Line two half-sheet pans with parchment paper.

Put the granulated sugar in a small bowl. Working with half of the dough at a time, break off 12 equal pieces and shape each piece into a small ball. Roll each ball around in the bowl of sugar; repeat with the remaining dough.

Place the balls on the prepared pans. Dip the bottom of a glass into the sugar, and press it down on each cookie until it flattens into a ¼- to ½-inch-thick circle. Bake for 12 to 14 minutes, or until the tops of the cookies feel set to the touch. Cool completely on wire racks.

PIZZETTES

Grace Rizzo

The Rizzos were my grandparents' dearest friends. Born in Sicily in the late 1800s, the two couples were lifelong neighbors, both in the old country and in America. Pizzettes is one of Mrs. Rizzo's famous cookie recipes that she brought with her from Italy. Thankfully, she shared this treasure with her daughters, Christine and Santa. · MAKES ABOUT 50 COOKIES

2½ tablespoons unsalted butter

9 ounces semisweet chocolate

1 cup granulated sugar

3 large eggs

Good squeeze from 1 lemon

½ cup milk

1 teaspoon ground cinnamon

1 teaspoon ground cloves

1 tablespoon baking powder

½ cup Dutch-process cocoa powder

4 cups all-purpose flour

8 ounces blanched almonds (skins removed), toasted and crushed (not fine and not too chunky)

Preheat the oven to 350°F. Line two half-sheet pans with parchment paper.

In the top of a double boiler, melt the butter and chocolate. Set aside to cool.

In the bowl of a stand mixer fitted with the paddle attachment, beat the sugar and eggs until pale yellow and thickened, about 2 minutes. Stir in the chocolate mixture, then the lemon juice and milk. Add the cinnamon, cloves, baking powder, cocoa, and flour. Mix just until combined. Fold in the almonds.

This is a sticky dough. With oiled hands, roll out a small portion to form a rope the thickness of a sausage. Flatten the dough slightly. Cut 1-inch-wide pieces, at an angle, and place on the prepared pans. Repeat this process with the remaining dough. Bake for about 10 minutes. Cool completely on wire racks.

2 tablespoons instant coffee

¼ cup boiling water

1 ounce semisweet chocolate

1 tablespoon unsalted butter

3 tablespoons Dutch-process cocoa
  powder

1 pound confectioners' sugar

Stir the coffee into the boiling water, and set aside.

In the top of a double boiler, melt the chocolate and butter. Remove from the heat, and add the cocoa, coffee mixture, and confectioners' sugar. Mix well.

Frost the cooled cookies.

CARROT CAKE COOKIES WITH GINGER CREAM CHEESE FROSTING

Amar Santana of Charlie Palmer at Bloomingdale's South Coast Plaza

Although Chef Santana has always had a sweet tooth and a passion for pastry, he signed up for the culinary program at the Culinary Institute of America on a full scholarship awarded by C-CAP. In 2001 Chef Charlie Palmer took him under his wing and has been his mentor ever since. One of the most important things that Chef Palmer taught him is that a true chef should be able to make everything, including dessert. This recipe combines two favorite confections—carrot cake and cookies. · MAKES ABOUT 40 COOKIES

½ cup pecans

2 cups all-purpose flour

1 tablespoon baking powder

2 teaspoons baking soda

8 ounces (2 sticks) unsalted butter, softened

½ cup packed light brown sugar

3 large eggs

1 teaspoon ground nutmeg

½ teaspoon ground allspice

1 teaspoon ground cinnamon

2 teaspoons ground ginger

½ cup grated carrots

½ cup golden raisins

¼ cup unsweetened shredded coconut

Preheat the oven to 325°F. Line two half-sheet pans with parchment paper.

Spread the pecans in a single layer on one of the prepared pans. Bake for 6 to 8 minutes, or until the nuts are lightly browned and fragrant. Cool completely in the pan, and set aside. Also set the pan aside, keeping the parchment paper, because you will need two pans to bake the cookies.

Mix the flour, baking powder, and baking soda in a large bowl, and set aside.

In the bowl of a stand mixer fitted with the paddle attachment, cream the butter and brown sugar. Add the eggs, one at a time, and mix until well incorporated. Mix in the nutmeg, allspice, cinnamon, and ginger. Gradually add the flour mixture, and mix just until incorporated. Fold in the carrots, raisins, coconut, and pecans.

Drop by rounded tablespoons, about 2 inches apart, onto the prepared pans. Bake for 12 to 15 minutes, or until the edges are lightly browned and cookies are set. Cool for 2 minutes, then remove to wire racks to cool completely.

GINGER CREAM CHEESE FROSTING

4 ounces cream cheese, softened

4 ounces (1 stick) unsalted butter, softened

2½ cups confectioners' sugar

¼ cup finely chopped crystallized ginger

1 teaspoon ground ginger

1 tablespoon spiced dark rum

1 teaspoon pure vanilla extract

½ teaspoon salt

In the bowl of a stand mixer fitted with the whip attachment, beat the cream cheese and butter until creamy. With the mixer on low speed, beat in the confectioners' sugar, ½ cup at a time, so that the sugar doesn't fly all over the place. Increase the speed to medium-high, and beat until light and fluffy. Add the crystallized ginger, ground ginger, rum, vanilla, and salt, beating until well mixed.

Spread the frosting on the tops of the cooled cookies.

PUMPKIN-MAPLE WALNUT COOKIES

Terrance Brennan of Artisanal

Chef Brennan sent me this recipe on the first crisp, cool day of autumn. He loves that time of year because of the abundance of seasonal ingredients available at the market and local farms. This cake-like sweet cookie with a hint of spice calls for pumpkin, a universal fall favorite. · MAKES ABOUT 24 COOKIES

2 cups all-purpose flour

1 tablespoon baking soda

½ teaspoon ground cinnamon

½ teaspoon ground ginger

½ teaspoon salt

10 ounces (2½ sticks) unsalted butter, softened

1½ cups packed dark brown sugar

1 teaspoon pure vanilla extract

2 large eggs

1 cup canned pumpkin puree

2 tablespoons molasses

1 cup walnuts

1 cup dried cranberries

Sift the flour, baking soda, cinnamon, ginger, and salt into a bowl, and set aside.

In a stand mixer fitted with the paddle attachment, cream the butter, brown sugar, and vanilla on medium-high speed for about 5 minutes. With a silicone spatula, scrape the bowl. Add the eggs, pumpkin puree, and molasses, and mix for 2 minutes. Scrape the bowl, add the flour mixture, and combine just until incorporated. Add the walnuts and cranberries, and mix for 1 minute. Form the dough into a disk and wrap in plastic wrap, and let it rest in the refrigerator for at least 3 hours, or up to 12 hours.

Preheat the oven to 325°F. Set aside two ungreased half-sheet pans.

On a lightly floured surface, roll out the dough to ⅛ inch thick. Cut out rounds using a 3-inch cookie cutter. Transfer the cookies to the pans. Bake for 4 minutes, then rotate the pan and bake for 4 more minutes. Cool completely on wire racks.

GRAHAM COOKIES

Alex Grunert of Blue Hill at Stone Barns

Graham cookies are a sophisticated take on the ubiquitous childhood honey graham crackers. This recipe, and the others by Chef Grunert, call for heirloom flours from Anson Mills. You will also need blood orange confit (fruit preserved in sugar), which is difficult to find in America, even at fancy food stores. Candied orange peel is a great substitute. • MAKES ABOUT 65 COOKIES

1¼ cups all-purpose flour

1 teaspoon baking powder

½ teaspoon baking soda

¼ teaspoon salt

1¼ cups Anson Mills graham flour

6½ tablespoons unsalted butter, softened

½ cup granulated sugar

¼ cup packed light brown sugar

¼ teaspoon ground cinnamon

½ cup honey

1 large egg

¼ cup milk

Grated zest of 1 lemon

1 teaspoon pure vanilla extract

¼ cup blood orange confit or candied orange peel, cubed (optional)

Sift together the all-purpose flour, baking powder, baking soda, and salt into a medium bowl. Stir in the graham flour, and set aside.

In the bowl of a stand mixer fitted with the paddle attachment, mix the butter, granulated sugar, brown sugar, cinnamon, and honey. Add the egg, milk, lemon zest, and vanilla. Cream until light and fluffy. Add the flour mixture, just until combined. With a silicone spatula, add the orange confit or peel (if using).

Line three half-sheet pans with parchment paper. Fill a piping bag fitted with a large plain tip with dough. Pipe small domes onto the prepared pans. Cover with plastic wrap, and let rest in the refrigerator for 1 hour.

Preheat the oven to 350°F.

Remove the pans from the refrigerator. Bake for about 7 minutes. Cool completely on wire racks.

CORN COOKIES
Alex Grunert of Blue Hill at Stone Barns

With a respect for artisanal ingredients, Chef Grunert uses a combination of ground corn, fresh lemon, and an abundance of butter to make these scrumptious cookies. They have a wonderful flavor due to their sweetness and the hint of citrus. · MAKES ABOUT 100 COOKIES

1 cup all-purpose flour

1 cup pastry flour

1 cup Anson Mills medium-coarse
   ground corn

½ teaspoon baking soda

1 teaspoon baking powder

2 teaspoons salt

Grated zest of 1 lemon

1 pound (4 sticks) unsalted butter,
   softened

2½ cups granulated sugar

2 large eggs

1½ teaspoons pure vanilla extract

Confectioners' sugar for sprinkling

Preheat the oven to 325°F. Line four half-sheet pans with parchment paper.

Combine the all-purpose flour, pastry flour, ground corn, baking soda, baking powder, salt, and lemon zest in a medium bowl, and set aside.

In the bowl of a stand mixer fitted with the paddle attachment, cream the butter and sugar. Combine the eggs with the vanilla, and add slowly to the creamed batter. Add the flour mixture, and mix just until combined.

Using a tablespoon-size ice-cream scoop, drop the batter onto the prepared pans, spacing the cookies 2 inches apart. (They are very buttery and will run together if placed too closely together.) Bake for 5 minutes. Turn the pans in the oven, and bake for another 5 minutes. Cool completely on wire racks. Sprinkle confectioners' sugar on top of the cooled cookies.

RED FIFE AND PUMPKIN SEED COOKIES
Alex Grunert of Blue Hill at Stone Barns

Chef Grunert shares another inventive cookie recipe that utilizes interesting ingredients, such as red fife flour, a hard wheat grain that imparts a nutty flavor. Buttery, lemony, and sweet, these cookies are easy to prepare.

• MAKES ABOUT 80 SMALL COOKIES

1 cup all-purpose flour

2 cups Anson Mills red fife flour

1 teaspoon baking powder

½ teaspoon baking soda

2 teaspoons salt

Grated zest of 1 lemon

8 ounces (2 sticks) unsalted butter,
    softened

2 cups granulated sugar

2 large eggs

1½ teaspoons pure vanilla extract

½ cup pumpkin seeds

Confectioners' sugar for sprinkling

Preheat the oven to 325°F. Line four half-sheet pans with parchment paper.

Combine the all-purpose flour, red fife flour, baking powder, baking soda, salt, and lemon zest in a medium bowl, and set aside.

In the bowl of a stand mixer fitted with the paddle attachment, cream the butter and sugar. Combine the eggs with the vanilla and add slowly to the creamed batter. With a silicone spatula, fold in the flour mixture and mix just until combined.

Using a tablespoon-size ice-cream scoop, drop the batter onto the prepared pans, spacing the cookies 2 inches apart. (They are very buttery and will run if placed too closely together.) Press the pumpkin seeds onto the cookies. Bake for 5 minutes. Turn the pans in the oven and bake for 5 more minutes. Cool completely on wire racks. Sprinkle confectioners' sugar on top of the cooled cookies.

LEMON-POPPY SEED LINZERS

Jennifer McCoy of Craft

Pastry chef McCoy developed this delightful recipe many years ago after a trip to Austria. She recalled, "I hopped from bakery to bakery sampling the many beautiful and delicious Viennese sweets—particularly the linzer cookies. These little shortbread sandwich cookies filled with a dollop of jam or marmalade became my favorite breakfast, alongside a strong cup of *kaffee*." She was inspired to combine her favorite lemon-poppy seed muffin with a traditional linzer to create this unique cookie. The sweetness marries perfectly with the tart, lemon curd filling. • MAKES ABOUT 30 BITE-SIZE SANDWICH COOKIES

POPPY SEED SHORTBREAD

6 ounces (1½ sticks) unsalted butter, softened	½ teaspoon pure vanilla extract
¼ cup granulated sugar	1¾ cups all-purpose flour
¼ cup confectioners' sugar, plus more for dusting	¼ teaspoon salt
	2 tablespoons poppy seeds

In the bowl of a stand mixer fitted with the paddle attachment, cream the butter, granulated sugar, confectioners' sugar, and vanilla on medium speed until light and fluffy. Reduce the speed to low and slowly add the flour and salt. Continue to mix until well incorporated. Slowly add the poppy seeds, and mix for about 1 minute.

Remove the dough from the mixer and place between 2 large sheets of parchment paper. Roll the dough to about ¼ inch thick. Remove the top layer of parchment and score the dough using a 1¼-inch round cookie cutter. To make the tops of the cookie sandwiches, score the centers of half of the rounds with a ½-inch round cookie cutter. Put the parchment back on top and gently slide the sheet of dough onto a half-sheet pan. Place in the freezer to chill for about 1 hour. (The dough can be prepared several days in advance.)

LEMON CURD FILLING

1 large egg

6 large egg yolks

½ cup granulated sugar

½ cup fresh lemon juice
   (about 4 lemons)

Finely grated zest of 2 lemons

Pinch of salt

4 ounces (1 stick) unsalted butter,
   softened

Fill a medium saucepan, about halfway full, with water, and bring to a boil. Reduce the heat to a simmer.

Fill a large bowl with ice water, and set aside.

Whisk together the egg, egg yolks, sugar, lemon juice, lemon zest, and salt in a large metal mixing bowl, and set over the saucepan of boiling water, ensuring that the bottom of the bowl is not touching the water. Whisk the mixture constantly until it reaches 170°F. Immediately remove the bowl from the heat, add the butter, and whisk until smooth. Strain the mixture though a fine-mesh sieve into another metal mixing bowl. Place over the bowl of ice water. Let the mixture stand at room temperature until cool and thickened.

Preheat the oven to 325°F. Line three half-sheet pans with parchment paper.

Remove the dough from the freezer and pop out the rounds of cut cookie dough. Arrange on the prepared pans, about ½ inch apart. Bake for 8 to 10 minutes, or until light golden brown. Cool completely on wire racks. Dust the tops of the cookies with confectioners' sugar. Pipe about ½ teaspoon lemon curd onto each cookie base, and gently sandwich with a cookie top.

CHAPTER

№ *6*

SUGAR COOKIES,

SHORTBREAD,

AND

DOUGHNUTS

JAMMY DODGERS

Michael Hartnell of Le Caprice at The Pierre

Jammy dodgers are a popular British "biscuit" made of shortbread cookies with jam sandwiched between them. Chef Hartnell's version calls for raspberry jam, but you may substitute any other flavor. These cookies are among the prettiest in this recipe collection. · MAKES 7 LARGE SANDWICH COOKIES

1½ cups all-purpose flour

1 teaspoon salt

1 tablespoon granulated sugar

½ teaspoon baking powder

½ teaspoon baking soda

7 tablespoons unsalted butter, softened

¼ cup plain yogurt

2 tablespoons milk

Raspberry jam, as needed

Confectioners' sugar for dusting (optional)

Preheat the oven to 375°F. Line two half-sheet pans with parchment paper.

In the bowl of a stand mixer fitted with the paddle attachment, combine the flour, salt, sugar, baking powder, and baking soda. Rub in the butter until the mixture is the consistency of bread crumbs. Add the yogurt and milk to form a rough dough. Do not overmix. Set aside, and allow the dough to rest for about 15 minutes.

Roll out the dough until it is about ½ inch thick. Cut out the dough with a 3-inch square cookie cutter. With a 1-inch round cookie cutter, cut out a small hole in half of the cookies. Place them all on the prepared pans.

Bake for 10 to 12 minutes, or until golden. Cool completely on wire racks. Turn over the cookies without the holes and pipe or spoon a dollop of jam onto each one. Dust the tops of the cookies with the holes with confectioners' sugar (if using), tapped through a small sieve. Sandwich the top and bottom cookie halves together, placing those with holes on the top.

TRAO-MAD WITH PEACH COMPOTE
Daniel Boulud of Café Boulud

I would happily munch on these cookies for breakfast, lunch, and dinner. Describing them, Chef Boulud says, "*Trao-Mad* are the tenderest, meltingest, butteryest cookies imaginable. They are the pride of the Brittany region of France, and they are delightfully, deliciously, and definitely addictive. At Café Boulud we serve them with a little bowl of peach compote and then change the compote as the seasons change, but *Trao-Mad* are also good with ice cream or sorbet, mousse, *pots de crèmes*, or solo—a plate of *Trao-Mad* and a cup of tea are always welcome." · MAKES ABOUT 32 COOKIES

PEACH COMPOTE

1½ pounds very ripe peaches

Freshly squeezed juice of ½ lemon

¼ cup honey

¼ cup water

Small pinch of saffron

Bring a large pot (a Dutch oven or saucepan is fine) of water to the boil. Plunge the peaches into the boiling water, blanch 30 seconds, then drain the peaches into a colander and run them under very cold water. When the fruit is cool enough to handle, peel the peaches and cut them in half along their "seams"; remove the pits. Set one peach (2 halves) aside and cut the remaining peaches into 1-inch cubes.

Put the cut-up peaches, the lemon juice, honey, and water in a medium saucepan over low-medium heat. Cook, stirring from time to time, 20 to 30 minutes, or until the peaches are so soft they fall apart when stirred. Add the saffron and cook, stirring frequently, 10 minutes more.

While the compote is cooking, cut the remaining peach into ¼-inch cubes and line a half-sheet pan with a large piece of plastic wrap.

When the compote is cooked, pull the pot from the heat and stir in the fresh peach cubes. Turn the compote out onto the plastic-lined half-sheet pan and spread it over the plastic in a thin layer. Top with the excess plastic wrap or another piece of plastic wrap, pressing the plastic against the compote to create an airtight seal. Chill in the refrigerator.

8 ounces (2 sticks) unsalted butter, softened

¾ cup plus 2 tablespoons confectioners' sugar, sifted

¼ teaspoon salt

2 large egg yolks

1⅓ cups all-purpose flour

⅓ cup almond flour or finely ground blanched almonds

1 large egg, lightly beaten, for the egg wash

Position the racks to divide the oven into thirds and preheat the oven to 400°F. Line two half-sheet pans with parchment paper.

Working in a mixer fitted with the paddle attachment (or in a bowl with a wooden spoon), beat the butter, sugar and salt together until they are creamy and smooth. Add the egg yolks and stir to blend. Add the all-purpose flour as well as the almond flour and continue to mix until the dough is homogeneous.

Using 1 tablespoon of dough for each cookie, drop the dough onto the prepared half-sheet pans leaving 1 inch of space between each dollop of dough. When all the dough is on the sheets, coat the tines of a fork with flour and use the back of the fork to make a crisscross pattern on the top of each cookie. Brush the cookies with a thin coating of egg wash and refrigerate the cookies, on the prepared pans, 1 hour.

Slide the pans into the oven and bake the cookies 8 to 10 minutes, or until they are a light golden brown. (If some of the cookies are browning faster than others, rotate the half-sheet pans front to back and top to bottom at the halfway point.) Using a wide metal spatula, transfer the cookies—still on the parchment paper—to a rack to cool to room temperature.

To serve: Spoon the compote into a small bowl and put the bowl on a large serving plate. Surround with cookies and serve, keeping a small jam spoon close by so that guests who are not dippers can spoon as much compote as they want onto each cookie.

SUGAR VALENTINES

Tracey Zabar

These cookies, sprinkled with coarse sugar, are elegant after-dinner sweets. This versatile dough can be rolled out and cut into any desired shape. Flower-shaped cookies are a lovely alternative to a pricey bouquet for your sweetie. Because these cookies are flat, you can also omit the sugar topping and decorate them with the icing of your choice. · MAKES ABOUT 60 SMALL COOKIES

8 ounces (2 sticks) unsalted butter, softened

1¾ cups granulated sugar

1 large egg

2 teaspoons pure vanilla extract

½ teaspoon salt

2¾ cups all-purpose flour

Sanding (coarse) or pearl sugar for sprinkling

Preheat the oven to 350°F. Line two half-sheet pans with parchment paper.

In the bowl of a stand mixer fitted with the paddle attachment, cream the butter and granulated sugar. Add the egg and vanilla and mix to combine. Gently fold in the salt and flour.

Roll out the dough between 2 large pieces of parchment paper until it is about ½ inch thick. Remove the top piece of parchment and, using a 1½-inch flower cookie cutter, cut out cookies and place them on the prepared pans. Sprinkle sanding or pearl sugar on top. Bake for 10 to 12 minutes, or until the edges of the cookies start to brown. Cool completely on wire racks.

ELI'S MOTHER'S BEST COOKIES
Eli Zabar of E.A.T.

Master baker Eli Zabar recalls that these cookies are the one memorable thing his mother, Lilly, ever made. In addition to being buttery and delicious, they are simple to prepare. • MAKES ABOUT 45 COOKIES

12 ounces (3 sticks) unsalted butter, softened

1 cup granulated sugar, plus extra for sprinkling

1 teaspoon pure vanilla extract

3½ cups all-purpose flour

¼ teaspoon salt

Preheat the oven to 350°F.

In the bowl of a stand mixer fitted with a paddle attachment, mix the butter and 1 cup of sugar together until just combined. Add the vanilla. Sift the flour and salt and add to the butter mixture. Mix on low speed until the dough starts to come together.

Turn the dough out onto a floured surface and shape into a flat disk, about 1 inch thick. Wrap in plastic wrap and chill for 30 minutes.

Roll the dough out less than ½ inch thick. Cut with cookie cutters. Eli's mother always punched out the cookies with a juice glass, but you can use whatever shape you want.

Place the cookies on two ungreased half-sheet pans and sprinkle with sugar. Bake for 20 to 25 minutes, until the edges just begin to show color. Cool completely on wire racks. Store in an airtight container.

PIZZELLE

Tracey Zabar

A pizzelle iron for making snowflake-shaped sugar cookies is a traditional gift for an Italian bride. Often the newlywed's initials are engraved into the iron plates so that her signature becomes part of the design. My Sicilian grandfather made these cookies with a long-handled iron that he held over the stove. Years later my mother was given the more efficient electric version. She followed the traditional recipe that came with the machine, but with one difference: Instead of using ½ teaspoon of anise extract, she tossed in the entire contents of the bottle, which perfumed the whole house and made these cookies oh-so-good.

• MAKES ABOUT 60 COOKIES

6 large eggs

1½ cups granulated sugar

8 ounces (2 sticks) unsalted butter, melted

One 1-ounce bottle pure anise extract (or 1 tablespoon pure vanilla extract)

3½ cups all-purpose flour

4 teaspoons baking powder

Confectioners' sugar for dusting (optional)

Plug in the pizzelle maker to preheat. Set two forks and two wire racks next to it.

In the bowl of a stand mixer fitted with the paddle attachment, beat the eggs and sugar until the batter is thick and falls off the paddle in a ribbon. Add the melted butter and anise extract, and mix. Add the flour and baking powder, and fold in just until combined. The batter will be somewhat sticky.

Open the top of the pizzelle maker. Using a small scoop or a teaspoon, drop a small amount of batter onto the center of each of the grids. Pull the top down and wait for about 15 to 20 seconds, then open the top. If the cookies look golden brown, they are done. If they are too light, carefully close the lid again for a few more seconds.

Remove the cookies, using the two forks, and place one on each rack to cool. By the time you make the next two, those underneath will be sufficiently cooled. For a pretty finish, dust the tops of the cooled cookies with confectioners' sugar.

NOTE: There are special molds, made of wood or metal, to shape the cookies into ice-cream cones or tube-shaped cannoli shells. These shells are not the same as the traditional deep-fried ones but are still delicious. Immediately after removing the hot cookie from the maker, simply wrap it around one of the molds. Allow the cookie to cool a bit, then slip it off the mold. Cool completely on a wire rack, and fill with ice cream or cannoli cream. You can also drape a hot cookie on top of a rolling pin or a small glass turned upside down. As it cools, it will form into a *tuile* or cup shape. Fill with berries and sweetened ricotta.

THE BAKER MAN'S CLASSIC THUMBPRINT COOKIES

Seth Greenberg of Seth Greenberg's Just Desserts

Almost twenty years ago, Chef Greenberg took over his father's bakery, William Greenberg Jr. Desserts. When I had my fourth child, he sent me a gigantic pink box filled with wonderful brownies and thumbprint cookies. On the box he had scrawled: "These are not for your children. These are not for your husband. These are not for your guests. These are not for your babysitter. These are for you, Tracey." I ended up sharing some of these scrumptious classic cookies with my family anyway. • MAKES ABOUT 65 COOKIES

8 ounces (2 sticks) unsalted butter, softened

½ cup plus 1½ tablespoons granulated sugar

½ teaspoon pure vanilla extract

⅝ teaspoon salt

2 large egg yolks

2¼ cups all-purpose flour (see Note), sifted, plus more for the counter

About 8 ounces seedless raspberry jam

Preheat the oven to 350°F (convection or traditional). Line two half-sheet pans with parchment paper.

In the bowl of a stand mixer fitted with the paddle attachment, cream the butter and sugar until smooth. Add the vanilla and salt. Scrape the mixture off the sides of the bowl and beater, and continue mixing. Add the egg yolks, one at a time, to the mixture while beating. Allow each to incorporate thoroughly. Scrape again. Mix until smooth. Add the flour. Stop and start the mixer to incorporate the flour, and then run on slow speed until the batter becomes a dough. The dough should pull away from the bottom of the mixing bowl but will not form a traditional ball due to the use of the paddle attachment instead of a dough hook.

Place the dough on a lightly floured surface. Knead by hand to check for uniformity. Roll out the dough to a thickness of ⅝ inch. It is helpful to use dowels or the equivalent as guides for your rolling pin to assure uniform thickness. Cut cookies approximately 1¼ inches in diameter, and place on the prepared pans, splitting the cookies evenly between the two sheets. Collect the scraps, knead together, reroll, and continue cutting cookies until all the dough is used.

Depress the center of each cookie using the rounded end of a wooden spoon handle or equivalent. Dip the end of the handle in flour periodically to prevent it from sticking. Make your depressions deep and straight, as shallow holes do not hold enough jam. Using a small pastry bag fitted with a decorating tip (such as Ateco #4), fill each depression generously with raspberry jam.

Bake for 20 to 25 minutes (or less if using a convection oven), or until golden brown on the bottom. Cool completely on wire racks.

NOTE: The amount of flour will vary depending on heat and humidity. The warmer and more humid it is, the more flour you will need.

PUNITIONS
Dorie Greenspan

Baking chronicler Dorie Greenspan gave me this charming French cookie recipe. She writes, "These grandmother cookies with rickrack edges are offered at Boulangerie Poilâne in Paris, piled in a basket. The late Lionel Poilâne, master artisan baker, told of grannies from his native Normandy who would tuck these sweet cookies behind their backs and, with a smile, would tease little ones to come take their punishments (*punitions*). Needless to say, the lucky children never had to be asked twice." · MAKES ABOUT 50 COOKIES

5 ounces (1¼ sticks) unsalted butter, softened
Slightly rounded ½ cup granulated sugar

1 large egg, at room temperature
2 cups all-purpose flour

Put the butter in the work bowl of a food processor fitted with the metal blade and process, scraping down the sides of the bowl as needed, until the butter is smooth. Add the sugar and process and scrape until thoroughly blended into the butter. Add the egg and continue to process, scraping the bowl as needed, until the mixture is smooth and satiny. Add the flour all at once, then pulse 10 to 15 times, until the dough forms clumps and curds and looks like streusel.

Turn the dough out onto a work surface and gather it into a ball. Divide the ball in half, shape each half into a disk, and wrap the disks in plastic. If you have the time, chill the disks until they are firm, about 4 hours. If you're in a hurry, you can roll the dough out immediately; it will be a little stickier, but fine. (The dough can be wrapped airtight and refrigerated for up to 4 days or frozen for up to 1 month.)

Position the racks to divide the oven into thirds and preheat the oven to 350°F. Line two half-sheet pans with parchment paper.

Working with one disk at a time, roll the dough out on a lightly floured surface until it is between ⅛ and ¼ inch thick. Using a 1½-inch round cookie cutter, cut out as many cookies as you can and place them on the prepared pans, leaving about 1 inch space between them. (You can gather the scraps into a disk and chill them, then roll, cut, and bake them later.)

Bake the cookies for 8 to 10 minutes, or until they are set but still pale. (If some of the cookies are thinner than others, the thin ones may brown around the edges. M. Poilâne would have approved. He'd tell you the spots of color here and there show they are made by hand.) Transfer the cookies to cooling racks to cool to room temperature.

The cookies can be kept in a tin at room temperature for about 5 days or wrapped airtight and frozen for up to 1 month.

DORIE'S GRANDMOTHER'S COOKIES
To make these cookies more like her grandmother's, brush each cut-out cookie with a little egg wash (1 egg beaten with 1 teaspoon cold water), then sprinkle the tops with sugar, cinnamon sugar, or poppy seeds before baking.

SOFT SUGAR CUTOUTS

Jen Shelbo of Maialino

Delicate cutouts are a part of pastry chef Shelbo's family's holiday tradition. Reminiscing about her childhood, she recalls making and decorating them for Christmas. "Every year I looked forward to helping my mom roll out the dough and cut out the cookies. But the best part was always eating the finished piece—a cakey cookie with a brightly colored, sugary frosting."

• MAKES ABOUT 80 SMALL COOKIES

5½ cups all-purpose flour
1 teaspoon baking soda
1 teaspoon baking powder
3 large eggs, well beaten
1 cup sour cream

8 ounces (2 sticks) unsalted butter, softened
2 cups granulated sugar
1 teaspoon salt
1 teaspoon pure vanilla extract
1 teaspoon pure almond extract

Combine the flour, baking soda, and baking powder in a large bowl, and set aside.

In a small bowl, mix together the eggs and sour cream.

In the bowl of a stand mixer fitted with the paddle attachment, cream the butter, sugar, salt, and vanilla and almond extracts. Mixing on low speed, add one-quarter of the flour mixture to the creamed mixture. Follow with one-third of the sour cream mixture. Repeat this procedure until all the ingredients are fully incorporated. Form the dough into a disk, and wrap in plastic wrap. Chill in the refrigerator overnight, or for at least 3 hours.

Preheat the oven to 425°F. Line two half-sheet pans with parchment paper.

On a well-floured surface, roll out the dough until very thin, about ¼ inch thick. Cut with your favorite cookie cutters and place the cutouts on the prepared pans. Bake for 8 to 10 minutes, or until the edges begin to turn a very light brown. Cool completely on wire racks. Frost with your favorite icing.

KOURAMBIETHES

Michelle Tampakis of the Institute of Culinary Education

These almond shortbread cookies were a favorite of pastry chef Tampakis's father, who had a sweet tooth and always wanted a little confection with fruit after dinner. Chef Tampakis explains their origin: "The *kourambiethes* are traditional cookies for any kind of celebration. Piled high with powdered sugar, they are the pride of many a Greek mother at their children's baptisms and weddings."

• MAKES ABOUT 70 COOKIES

12 ounces (3 sticks) unsalted butter, softened
½ cup confectioners' sugar, plus sifted confectioners' sugar for garnish
4 large egg yolks

¼ cup brandy
½ teaspoon pure vanilla extract
1¾ cups almond flour
4 cups all-purpose flour

Preheat the oven to 300°F. Line two half-sheet pans with parchment paper.

In the bowl of a stand mixer fitted with the paddle attachment, cream the butter and sugar until very light and fluffy, 7 to 10 minutes. Add the egg yolks one at a time, stopping often to scrape down the bowl. Add the brandy, vanilla, and almond flour. Gradually add the all-purpose flour, until a soft, pliable dough is formed. Remove the dough from the bowl and knead gently with your hands to make smooth.

Using about 2 tablespoons of dough for each cookie, shape the dough into half moons or disks. Space the cookies about ½ inch apart on the prepared pans. Bake for about 30 minutes, or until lightly colored. Cool completely on wire racks, and then dredge generously with confectioners' sugar.

GRANNY RENNIE'S SCOTTISH SHORTBREAD

Mark Tasker of Balthazar

Pastry chef Tasker's Granny Rennie was known for her shortbread cookies. During the Second World War, she made them as a treat for her six children when they had to go into the air-raid shelter. (Chef Tasker wonders how the children ate them when they were supposed to be wearing gas masks.) His granny used a wooden stamp to mark the cookies with a thistle design. She also left the dough outdoors overnight in the cold climate of Scotland, but you should use your refrigerator. · MAKES ABOUT 50 COOKIES

1 pound (4 sticks) unsalted butter, softened

⅔ cup packed light brown sugar

1 cup confectioners' sugar

¾ teaspoon salt

5 cups all-purpose flour

In the bowl of a stand mixer fitted with the paddle attachment, cream the butter, brown sugar, and confectioners' sugar until light and airy. Add the salt and flour, and mix just until combined. Form the dough into a disk, wrap in plastic wrap, and refrigerate overnight.

Preheat the oven to 270°F. Line two half-sheet pans with parchment paper.

Remove the dough from the refrigerator. Roll out very thin, about ¼ inch thick, and cut with a 2-inch cookie cutter. Place the cutouts on the prepared pans. Bake for about 20 minutes. Cool completely on wire racks.

BUGNES DE LYON
Daniel Boulud of Daniel

Chef Boulud gave me this recipe for *bugnes*, which are closer to a cruller than a cookie. This version, one of his favorites, is typical of his hometown of Lyon. I love the image of his mother making them with a wooden spoon. The suggested beverages to accompany this sweet treat are a *verveine* (liqueur) infusion or an espresso with Cointreau on the side. · MAKES 20 TO 25 BUGNES

1½ tablespoons unsalted butter, softened
1 teaspoon granulated sugar
Pinch of salt
1 large egg
Grated zest of ½ navel orange

Rounded ¼ teaspoon baking powder
1 cup plus 2 tablespoons all-purpose flour
3 tablespoons whole milk
Peanut oil for deep-frying
Confectioners' sugar, for dusting

Using a wooden spoon (as my mother would) or working in a mixer fitted with the paddle attachment, beat the butter, sugar, and salt together until creamy. Add the egg and beat well, then beat in the orange zest. Stir the baking powder into the flour, and then stir the flour into the bowl alternately with the milk, incorporating the flour in three additions and the milk in two. Turn the dough out onto a counter—or just reach into the bowl—and knead the dough lightly to form it into a ball. Cover the dough with plastic wrap and chill it in the refrigerator for at least 1 hour, or, preferably, overnight.

Dust a half-sheet pan with flour and keep it close at hand. To shape the *bugnes* as my mother does, roll the dough out on a lightly floured work surface into a rectangle that's ¼ to ⅛ inch thick—these shouldn't be too thick. Cut the dough into 1-inch-wide strips and, using a sharp knife or a pastry cutter, cut each strip on the diagonal at 2-inch intervals—you'll have created diamonds. Now, cut a 1½-inch-long slit down the center of each piece of dough—the slit should run down the length of the diamond. Take the top or bottom corner of the dough and lift it up and into the slit, then pull it out the other side—you will have created a twisted, handkerchief-like knot. Place the *bugnes* on the floured half-sheet pan, cover them with plastic wrap, and refrigerate for 1 hour.

Pour at least 4 inches of oil into a deep pot and heat it to 350°F, as measured on a deep-fat thermometer. Line a half-sheet pan with a double thickness of paper towels and keep the pan and a slotted spoon close at hand.

Drop 5 to 6 *bugnes* into the oil—you don't want to crowd the pot—and fry for about 2 minutes, or until the underside of each is golden. Turn them over and fry for another 2 minutes or so, just until the second side is also golden. Lift the *bugnes* out of the oil with a slotted spoon and place them on the towel-lined pan to drain. Repeat with the remaining *bugnes*. Sprinkle the pastries generously with confectioners' sugar and serve while they're still warm.

RIBBON COOKIES

Jerry Thornton of SD26

Chef Thornton's fanciful doughnut-like cookie recipe goes back to his great-grandparents in Italy. He explains, "Our family would all gather around in the kitchen for holidays and make these in a gigantic batch to give to friends, teachers, and family. We sat up on stools, tying knots, while my parents rolled the dough and fried them. This recipe is my first memory of baking. You can substitute another citrus zest for the orange zest, and the extract can change to any liquid you might desire" • MAKES ABOUT 30 COOKIES

CINNAMON SUGAR

1 cup granulated sugar   1 tablespoon ground cinnamon

Mix the sugar with the cinnamon in a medium bowl, and set aside.

12 ounces (3 sticks) unsalted butter,   2½ tablespoons baking powder
   softened   1 teaspoon pure almond extract
1 cup granulated sugar   Grated zest of ½ orange
6 large eggs   6 cups all-purpose flour, as needed
¼ cup milk   Vegetable oil for frying
¼ teaspoon salt

In the bowl of a stand mixer fitted with the paddle attachment, cream the butter and sugar. Add the eggs, milk, salt, and baking powder. The mixture will look broken. Let stand for 15 minutes.

Add the almond extract and orange zest, and continue beating. Add the flour in 1-cup increments until the dough is smooth, shiny, and no longer sticky. You may need to use slightly more or less of the required 6 cups of flour.

Line a large bowl with paper towels and set beside the stove. Heat the vegetable oil in a large, deep pot or electric skillet to 375°F.

Roll small pieces of the dough into circles that are about 8 inches in diameter, and cut into ¾-inch strips with a pastry cutter. Tie each strip into a knot, and fry until golden brown. Drain the cookies in the paper towel-lined bowl, and toss in cinnamon sugar.

BRAIDS
Grace Rizzo

This century-old recipe comes from the little hill town of San Piero Patti, in Sicily, where my grandfather grew up. The cookies are from his dear friend and neighbor, Grace. The doughnut-like braids are deep-fried in oil, then dipped in sweet, lemony syrup. Grated chocolate is then sprinkled on top.

• MAKES ABOUT 20 BRAIDS

SYRUP

2 cups granulated sugar

1¼ cups water

Grated zest of 1 lemon

Bittersweet or semisweet chocolate
   for garnish

Place the sugar, water, and lemon zest in a medium saucepan and bring to a boil. Continue boiling until the syrup thickens, which will allow the flavors to fuse. Cool completely and set aside. Reserve the chocolate for garnish.

3 tablespoons unsalted butter,
   softened

3 tablespoons granulated sugar

4 large eggs, slightly beaten

¼ cup water

Pinch of salt

5 cups all-purpose flour

Canola oil for frying

In the bowl of a stand mixer fitted with the paddle attachment, mix the butter and sugar. (You can also mix by hand, using a wooden spoon and a large bowl.) Add the eggs and water and combine well, then add the salt and flour. Change to the dough hook attachment, and knead the dough until it is smooth.

   Set a slotted spoon and a half-sheet pan that is lined with paper towels next to the stove.

   In a deep pot, heat 4 or 5 inches of the canola oil to 350°F, as measured on a deep-fat thermometer.

Divide the dough into 3 pieces. Working quickly so that it doesn't dry out, roll the first piece with a rolling pin until it is very thin, about ⅜ inch thick and about 7 inches wide. (You can also use a pasta machine: Put the dough through the #1 setting, then through the #5 setting.) With a pastry cutter, cut strips that are about 7 inches long by 1¼ inches wide. Form a cross with 2 strips and twist them to form a braid. Repeat with the rest of the strips; then repeat the process with the other 2 pieces of dough.

Place the braids carefully in the hot oil and cook until golden brown on both sides. Drain on the paper towel-lined pan.

Dip the cooled braids, one at a time, into the syrup. Hold each braid over the saucepan to let the syrup drain back into the pan. Place each braid on a serving platter. Shave the reserved chocolate, and sprinkle over the platter of braids.

CENCI

Sirio Maccioni of Le Cirque

Restaurateur Sirio Maccioni's favorite Italian cookies are his wife, Egi's, Tuscan fried-dough bows. These light fritters are traditionally made for Carnevale, or Fat Tuesday, the last day before Lent. · MAKES ABOUT 12 COOKIES

3 tablespoons butter, softened

2 tablespoons granulated sugar

Grated zest of 1 lemon (about
    ½ teaspoon)

3 large egg yolks

2 tablespoons milk

2 tablespoons Sambuca (anise-flavored
    liqueur)

1½ tablespoons pure vanilla extract

2½ cups all-purpose flour

Milk, if needed

Vegetable oil for deep-frying

¼ cup confectioners' sugar for
    finishing

Combine the butter, sugar, and lemon zest in a food processor. Add the egg yolks, one at a time, pulsing to combine well after each. Add the milk, Sambuca, and vanilla. Mix well. Add the flour. Combine well until you have a soft and crumbly dough. Add a few drops of milk if the dough is too dry.

Heat the vegetable oil in a deep pot. Line a half-sheet pan with paper towels and set next to the stove.

Roll out the dough into a rectangle 8 inches wide, about 12 inches long, and ⅛ inch thick. Cut the dough into 8 by 1-inch strips, using a knife or a pastry wheel. Carefully twist the strips into loose knots. Deep-fry the knots in hot oil until they begin to turn golden brown. Remove from oil to the paper towel-lined pan. Sprinkle immediately and abundantly with confectioners' sugar. Serve the *cenci* warm.

COFFEE AND DOUGHNUT COOKIES

Heather Bertinetti of Convivio

Chef Bertinetti came up with the brilliant idea of putting two breakfast treats inside one cookie. She told me, "I love coffee and doughnuts for breakfast, but I can't always find time to eat. I figured, why not combine the two into a delicious cookie I can munch on all day long." • MAKES ABOUT 100 COOKIES

12 ounces doughnut holes

12 ounces (3 sticks) unsalted butter, softened

1 cup granulated sugar

2½ cups packed light brown sugar

1 tablespoon instant espresso powder

½ teaspoon pure vanilla extract

3 large eggs

⅓ cup corn syrup

4½ cups all-purpose flour

½ teaspoon baking soda

½ teaspoon salt

Preheat the oven to 350°F. Line three half-sheet pans with parchment paper.

Cut the doughnut holes in quarters and set aside.

In the bowl of a stand mixer fitted with the paddle attachment, cream the butter, granulated sugar, brown sugar, and espresso powder until light and fluffy. In a small bowl, combine the vanilla with the eggs, whisking gently with a fork. Add this mixture slowly to the batter, then add the corn syrup. Add the flour, baking soda, and salt, and mix just until combined.

With a silicone spatula, add the doughnut holes and fold in gently.

Scoop tablespoon-size balls onto the prepared pans. Bake for 6 to 8 minutes. Cool completely on wire racks before glazing.

COFFEE GLAZE

2½ cups confectioners' sugar

½ cup freshly brewed espresso

With a silicone spatula, mix the confectioners' sugar and espresso until combined and all the lumps are gone.

Dip the tops of the cookies in the glaze and dry the cookies on wire racks.

TRACEY'S BOOKSHELF

Many of the *One Sweet Cookie* participants, in addition to being chefs and bakers, are also authors. Here are my favorite books by this accomplished crew, along with a few others. These titles are the ones in my library that I return to often for recipes and ideas or for a pleasurable read.

Allen, Ida Bailey. *The Modern Method of Preparing Delightful Foods*. New York: Corn Products Refining Co., 1929.

Bastianich, Lidia Matticchio and Tanya Bastianich Manuali. *Lidia's Italy: 140 Simple and Delicious Recipes From the Ten Places in Italy Lidia Loves Most*. New York: Alfred A. Knopf, 2007.

Batali, Mario. *Holiday Food*. New York: Clarkson Potter/Publishers, 2000.

Batchelder, Ann. *New Delineator Recipes*. Chicago: John F. Cuneo Company, 1930.

Beeton, Mrs. *Mrs. Beeton's Every Day Cookery*. London: Ward, Lock & Co., Limited, 1912.

Berolzheimer, Ruth, Editor. *The American Woman's Cookbook*. Chicago: Consolidated Book Publishers, Inc., 1942.

Boulud, Daniel. *Cooking with Daniel Boulud*. New York: Random House, Inc., 1993.

Brennan, Terrance and Andrew Friedman. *Artisanal Cooking: A Chef Shares His Passion for Handcrafting Great Meals at Home*. Hoboken: John Wiley & Sons, Inc., 2005.

Callen, Anna Teresa. *Food and Memories of Abruzzo: Italy's Pastoral Land*. Hoboken: John Wiley & Sons, Inc., 1998.

Casella, Cesare. *True Tuscan: Flavors and Memories from the Countryside of Tuscany*. New York: HarperCollins Publishers, 2005.

Child, Julia, *The Way to Cook*. New York: Alfred A. Knopf, 1989.

Choate, Judith. *The Fundamental Techniques of Classic Pastry Arts: The French Culinary Institute*. New York: Stewart, Tabori & Chang, 2009.

Cunningham, Marion. *The Fannie Farmer Baking Book*. New York: Gramercy Publishing, 1996.

DeMasco, Karen and Mindy Fox. *The Craft of Baking: Cakes, Cookies and Other Sweets with Ideas for Inventing Your Own*. New York: Clarkson Potter/Publishers, 2009.

English, Todd, Paige Retus, and Sally Sampson. *The Olives Dessert Table: Spectacular Restaurant Desserts You Can Make at Home*. New York: Simon & Schuster, Inc., 2000.

Farmer, Fannie Merritt. *The Boston Cooking-School Cook Book*. Boston: Little, Brown, and Company, 1917.

Grammatico, Maria and Mary Taylor Simeti. *Bitter Almonds: Recollections and Recipes from a Sicilian Girlhood*. New York: William Morrow, 1994.

Grausman, Richard. *At Home with the French Classics*. New York: Workman Publishing Co., 1988.

Greenspan, Dorie. *Baking: From My Home to Yours*. New York: Houghton Mifflin Harcourt Publishing Company, 2006.

Gutenbrunner, Kurt with Jane Sigal. *Neue Cuisine: The Elegant Tastes of Vienna; Recipes from Wallsé, Café Sabarsky and Blaue Gans*. New York: Rizzoli International Publications, Inc., 2011.

Heatter, Maida. *Maida Heatter's Book of Great American Desserts*. New York: Alfred A. Knopf, 1985.

Keller, Thomas. *The French Laundry Cookbook*. New York: Artisan, 1999.

Levine, Sarabeth. *Sarabeth's Bakery: From My Hands to Yours*. New York: Rizzoli International Publications, Inc., 2010.

Lucas, Dione. *The Cordon Bleu Cook Book*. Boston: Little, Brown and Company, 1947.

Maccioni, Egi with Peter Kaminsky. *The Maccioni Family Cookbook: Recipes and Memories from an Italian-American Kitchen.* New York: Stewart, Tabori & Chang, 2003.

Malgieri, Nick. *Great Italian Desserts.* Boston: Little, Brown and Company, 1990.

Malouf, Waldy. *The Hudson River Valley Cookbook: A Leading American Chef Savors the Region's Bounty.* Boston: Harvard Common Press, 1998.

McCarty, Michael. *Michael's Cookbook: The Art of New American Food and Entertaining.* New York: Macmillan Publishing Company, 1989.

McNally, Keith, Riad Nasr, and Lee Hanson. *The Balthazar Cookbook.* New York: Clarkson Potter/ Publishers, 2003.

Meyer, Danny and Michael Romano. *The Union Square Cafe Cookbook: 160 Favorite Recipes from New York's Acclaimed Restaurant.* New York: HarperCollins Publishers, 1994.

Negrin, Micol. *Rustico: Regional Italian Country Cooking.* New York: Clarkson Potter/Publishers, 2002.

Ong, Pichet and Genevieve Ko. *The Sweet Spot: Asian-Inspired Desserts.* New York: William Morrow, 2007.

Palmer, Charlie. *Charlie Palmer's Casual Cooking: The Chef of New York's Aureole Restaurant Cooks for Family and Friends.* New York: HarperCollins Publishers, 2001.

Payard, François. *Simply Sensational Desserts: 140 Classics for the Home Baker from New York's Famous Patisserie and Bistro.* New York: Clarkson Potter/Publishers, 1999.

Peck, Paula. *The Art of Fine Baking.* New York: Simon & Schuster, Inc., 1961.

Ripert, Eric and Maguy Le Coze. *Le Bernardin Cookbook: Four-Star Simplicity.* New York: Clarkson Potter/Publishers, 1998.

Rubin, Maury. *Book of Tarts: Form, Function, and Flavor at the City Bakery.* New York: William Morrow, 1995.

Samuelsson, Marcus. *New American Table.* Hoboken: John Wiley & Sons, Inc., 2009.

Sax, Richard. *Classic Home Desserts: A Treasury of Heirloom and Contemporary Recipes from Around the World.* Shelburne, Vermont: Chapters Publishing, 1994.

Soltner, André. *The Lutèce Cookbook.* New York: Alfred A. Knopf, 1995.

Tong, Michael. *The Shun Lee Cookbook: Recipes from a Chinese Restaurant Dynasty.* New York: William Morrow, 2007.

Torres, Jacques and Judith Choate. *Jacques Torres' A Year in Chocolate: 80 Recipes for Holidays and Special Occasions.* New York: Stewart, Tabori & Chang, 2008.

Tourondel, Laurent and Charlotte March. *Fresh from the Market: Seasonal Cooking with Laurent Tourondel.* Hoboken: John Wiley & Sons, Inc., 2010.

Valenti, Tom and Andrew Friedman. *Welcome to My Kitchen: A New York Chef Shares His Robust Recipes and Secret Techniques.* New York: HarperCollins Publishers, 2002.

Vongerichten, Jean-Georges and Mark Bittman. *Cooking at Home with a Four-Star Chef.* New York: Broadway Books, 1998.

Wallace, Lily Haxworth. *The Lily Wallace New American Cook Book.* New York: Books, Inc., 1945.

Waxman, Jonathan. *A Great American Cook: Recipes from the Home Kitchen of One of Our Most Influential Chefs.* New York: Houghton Mifflin Harcourt Publishing Company, 2007.

White, Michael. *Fiamma: The Essence of Contemporary Italian Cooking.* Hoboken: John Wiley & Sons, Inc., 2006.

Woman's Institute of Domestic Arts and Sciences. *Recipes for Food to Sell.* Scranton: International Textbook Company, 1943.

ACKNOWLEDGMENTS

This book would not have been possible without the kindness and generosity of the chefs, pastry chefs, bakers, teachers, and restaurateurs who shared their favorite recipes with me. I also want to thank those who gave me invaluable encouragement and introduced me to other helpful individuals: Dan Barber, Wylie Dufresne, Katy Foley, Devon Fredericks, Ina Garten, David Glass, Lili Lynton, Tanya Bastianich Manuali, Alina Martell, Keith McNally, Danny Meyer, Steve Millington, Drew Nieporent, Charlie Palmer, Carmen Quagliata, Lauren Resler, Eric Ripert, Michael Romano, Michael Tong, Vera Tong, Michael White, and Alex Williamson. To my teachers, especially the French Culinary Institute's instructors—you have been an inspiration. And to the memory of Julia Child, who gave me wonderful advice once upon a time.

A special thank-you to Richard Grausman, founder and president of C-CAP, mentor, and friend. To everyone at Zabar's, especially Stanley, Saul, and Danny Zabar. And to Zabar's Gladys Garcia and David Lopez, who helped me locate hard-to-find ingredients and baking equipment.

I am also indebted to Sarah Abell, Molly Adams, Melissa Au-Yeung, Kate Betts, Christine Burgin, Mary Donlon, Courtney Dykstra, Lucinda East, Lauren Falk, Georgette Farkas, Lauren Fonda, Helen Freund, Shelby Goldman, Christina Grimsley, Liz Gutterson, Irene Hamburger, Grayson Handy, Robin Insley, Lindsey Jaffe, Anita Jaronik, Erin Jevis, Gina Kamburowski, Amanda Klein, Pamela Lewy, Ronna Lichtenberg, Alexandra Maxwell, Susan Morgenthau, Lindsey Myers, Aaron Oser, Mandy Oster, Chiara Sassoli, Jessie Schupack, Jane Stewart, Carolyn Thalin, Lindsey Valdez, Diana Van Buren, Brooke Vecchio, Allison Wagner, and Tamara Wood.

Thanks to everyone at Rizzoli: especially my endlessly talented and patient editor, Sandy Gilbert, and publisher, Charles Miers, and to Maria Pia Gramaglia, Jennifer Pierson, Christopher Steighner, Jono Jarrett, Kayleigh Jankowski, Hilary Ney, Deborah Weiss Geline, Ron Longe, Pam Sommers, Jessica Napp, Susan Homer, and Marilyn Flaig. To the rest of my amazing book team: photographer Ellen Silverman, stylist Lucy Attwater, graphic designer Jan Derevjanik, Mario De Palma, Samantha Napolitano, Barry Ohannessian, Kevin Norris, and Ali Castleman.

To my friends at the beach and in the city, who sampled countless cookies, and in particular, to the Shapiro, Butler, Eckstein, Levinson, and Ressler families. And to Randie and Carolyn Malinsky, Paula Semel, Elissa Sherwin, Pat Shepland, Vicki Waller, Jay Embree, Bernard Cohen, and Jon and Grace Lindsey. And most of all, to my baking companion, Alexandra Trower Lindsey.

To the memory of my mother, Mary, and godmother, Eleanor, who taught me to bake all things Sicilian style. To the rest of the Blumenreich and Zabar families, and to Marki Grimsley. With love to my husband, David, and children, Benjamin, Danny, Michael, William, and Mary Rose—this one is for you.

A portion of the proceeds from each book benefit Careers through Culinary Arts Program (C-CAP), which is a national nonprofit organization founded by Richard Grausman. C-CAP works with public high schools to prepare students for careers in the restaurant and hospitality industry and has awarded more than thirty million dollars in scholarships. www.ccapinc.org

SOURCES

ANSON MILLS
www.ansonmills.com
Heirloom flours, such as red fife and graham, and cornmeal.

BONNIE SLOTNICK COOKBOOKS
163 West 10th Street
New York, New York 10014
(212) 989-8962
www.bonnieslotnickcookbooks.com
A bookstore specializing in old and out-of-print cookbooks.

KALUSTYAN'S
123 Lexington Avenue
New York, New York 10016
(800) 352-3551
www.kalustyans.com
The go-to supplier for rare spices, including Mexican cinnamon.

KING ARTHUR FLOUR
135 Route 5 South
Norwich, Vermont 05055
(800) 827-6836
www.kingarthurflour.com
The baker's store for flour, yeast, English muffin rings, and pistachio paste.

ZABAR'S AND COMPANY
2245 Broadway
New York, New York 10024
(800) 697-6301
www.zabars.com
The ultimate source for all kinds of kitchen equipment and baking ingredients, including KitchenAid stand mixers, pizzelle makers, baking tools, vanilla sugar, King Arthur flour, Valrhona and Guittard chocolates, nuts, dried fruits, and spices.

U.S. AND METRIC CONVERSION CHARTS

All conversions are approximate.

WEIGHT CONVERSIONS

U.S.	METRIC
½ ounce	14 g
1 ounce	28 g
1½ ounces	43 g
2 ounces	57 g
2½ ounces	71 g
3 ounces	85 g
3½ ounces	100 g
4 ounces	113 g
5 ounces	142 g
6 ounces	170 g
7 ounces	200 g
8 ounces	227 g
9 ounces	255 g
10 ounces	284 g
11 ounces	312 g
12 ounces	340 g
13 ounces	368 g
14 ounces	400 g
15 ounces	425 g
1 pound	454 g

OVEN TEMPERATURES

°F	GAS MARK	°C
250	½	120
275	1	140
300	2	150
325	3	165
350	4	180
375	5	190
400	6	200
425	7	220
450	8	230
475	9	240
500	10	260
550	Broil	290

LIQUID CONVERSIONS

U.S.	METRIC
1 teaspoon	5 ml
1 tablespoon	15 ml
2 tablespoons	30 ml
3 tablespoons	45 ml
¼ cup	60 ml
⅓ cup	75 ml
⅓ cup plus 1 tablespoon	90 ml
⅓ cup plus 2 tablespoons	100 ml
½ cup	120 ml
⅔ cup	150 ml
¾ cup	180 ml
¾ cup plus 2 tablespoons	200 ml
1 cup	240 ml
1 cup plus 2 tablespoons	275 ml
1¼ cups	300 ml
1⅓ cups	325 ml
1½ cups	350 ml
1⅔ cups	375 ml
1¾ cups	400 ml
1¾ cups plus 2 tablespoons	450 ml
2 cups (1 pint)	475 ml
2½ cups	600 ml
3 cups	725 ml
4 cups (1 quart)	945 ml
(1,000 ml = 1 liter)	

INDEX

Page numbers in *italics* indicate illustrations.

Almond(s)
  Biscotti (*Biscotti alle Mandorle*),
    132–133, *133*
  Crescents of Cardamom and,
    57–58
  Florentine Cookies, *60*, 61
  Hungarian Crescents, Sugars', 54,
    55, 56
  Kipferl, *52*, 53
  Kourambiethes, 174
  Meringues (*Brutti Ma Buoni*), 116
  -Nutella Coconut Macaroons,
    122, 123
  Petits Fours de Noël, 101–102
  Pizzettes, 144–145
Almond Paste
  Hungarian Crescents, Sugar's,
    54, *55*, 56
  Pistachio Cookies, 120, *121*
  Tea Cakes, Pineapple, 47
Anís Bredele, 98, *99*
Anise
  Anís Bredele, 98, *99*
  Cenci, 182
  Petits Fours à l'Anise, 100
  Pizzelle, *164*, 165–166
Ansel, Dominique, 108
Apricot
  in Crescents of Almond and
    Cardamom, 57–58
  Rugelach, Quentin's Grandma's,
    92, 94
  in Tea Cakes, Pineapple, 47
Augendre, Ludovic, 118
Aumont, Marc, 61

Back-to-School Raspberry Granola
  Bars, 32–33, *33*
Baker Man's Classic Thumbprint
  Cookies, The, 167–168, *169*
Baking. *See also* Ingredients
  books on, 184–185
  equipment and tools, 10–11
  setup (*mise en place*), 13–14
Bali Hai Brownies, 21
Banana Chocolate Chip
  Sandwiches, *80*, 81
Bars and Squares. *See also* Brownies
  Chumleys, *24*, 25
  Fig Squares, 26, *27*, 28
  Jam Bars, 33

Lamington Bars, 29–30, *31*
Raspberry Granola Bars, Back-to-
  School, 32–33, *33*
Bastianich, Lidia, 49, 184
Batali, Benno, 86
Batali, Mario, 86, 184
Bellanger, Florian, 118
Bertinetti, Heather, 183
Biscotti
  Almond (*Biscotti alle Mandorle*),
    132–133, *133*
  Chocolate, Wicked, 130–131, *131*
  Fig and Walnut, Cinnamon-
    Scented, 128–129
Biscuits, Chocolate, 131
Bookshelf, baking, 184–185
Boulud, Daniel, 158, 176, 184
Braids, 180–181
Brennan, Terrance, 148, 184
Brownies
  Bali Hai, 21
  Cheesecake, 22, *23*
  Milk Chocolate, *16*, 17–18
  Milk Chocolate, Pecan, 18
  Palm Beach, with Chocolate-
    Covered Mints, 19–21
Brutti Ma Buoni, 116
Bugnes de Lyon, 176–177
Butter, 12–13
Butterscotch Chips, in Crazy
  Cowboy Cookies, 86, *87*

Cakey Cookies. *See also* Bars and
  Squares; Brownies
  Madeleines for Alex, 42, *43*
  Orange, *48*, 49–50
  Ricotta, *44*, 45–46
  Ricotta Chip, 46
  Ricotta Coconut Clouds, 46
  Ricotta Sammies, 46
  Snickerdoodles, *40*, 41
  Snickerdoodles, Lauren's, 39
  Sugar Cutouts, Soft, 172, *173*
  Tea Cakes, Pineapple, 47
  Whoopie Pies, 34–35
  Whoopie Pies, Red Velvet, *36*,
    37–38
Callen, Anna Teresa, 132, 184
Candied Peel. *See* Citrus Peel,
  Candied
Cardamom, Crescents of Almond
  and, 57–58
Carrot Cake Cookies with Ginger
  Cream Cheese Frosting, 146–147

Casella, Cesare, 116, 184
Cashew *Polvorones*, 62, *63*
Cenci, 182
Cheesecake Brownies, 22, *23*
Cherry
  -Pistachio Oatmeal Cookies,
    88, 89
  Surprise Cookies, 77
Chocolate. *See also* Brownies
  Biscotti, Wicked, 130–131, *131*
  Biscuits, 131
  Chocolate Chip Cookies
    (variation), 85
  Coconut Macaroons, -Dipped, 126
  Coconut Macaroons, -Drizzled,
    125
  coins (*pistoles*), 12
  Flourless Chocolate Cookies,
    104–105, *105*
  Frosting, 145
  Fudge Cookies, Double-Chocolate,
    106, 107
  Ganache, 30
  Juliet's Kisses, *110*, 111–112
  Knobs, 103
  Macadamia Cookies, Milk
    Chocolate-Peppermint, 68–69
  and Pecan Cookies, 108, *109*
  Pizzettes, 144–145
  in Romeo's Sighs and Juliet's
    Kisses, *110*, 111–112
  Rugelach, Quentin's Grandma's,
    92, 94–95
  tempered, 12
  weighing, 11
  Whoopie Pies, 34–35
  Whoopie Pies, Red Velvet, *36*,
    37–38
Chocolate Chip(s)
  Banana Sandwiches, *80*, 81
  in Cherry Surprise Cookies, 77
  in Chocolate Biscotti, Wicked,
    130–131, *131*
  in Chumleys, *24*, 25
  Coconut Cookies, 71, *72*, 73
  Cookies, 83, *84*, 85
  Cookies, Chocolate (variations), 85
  Everything Cookie, 82
  in Fudge Cookies, Double-
    Chocolate, *106*, 107
  homemade, 12
  Meringue Cookies, Mint,
    Nonny's, 117
  Monster Cookies, 74, *75*

in Oatmeal Raisin Cookies, City
    Bakery, 90
in Pecan and Chocolate Cookies,
    108, *109*
Ricotta Cookies, 46
in Sandys, 76
Triple Chocolate and Walnut
    Cookies, Todd's Favorite, 78, *79*
Chocolate Chunks
in Chocolate Knobs, 103
homemade, 12
Christmas Cookies
Anís Bredele, 98, *99*
Petits Fours de Noël, 101–102
Pistachio, 120, *121*
Sugar Cutouts, Soft, 172, *173*
Chumleys, *24*, 25
Cinnamon-Scented Fig and Walnut
    Biscotti, 128–129
Cinnamon Sugar, 178
Citrus Peel, Candied, 136
Cherry Surprise Cookies, 77
Florentine Cookies, *60*, 61
Ginger Citrus Cookies, *134*,
    135–136
Graham Cookies, 149
Sandys, 76
City Bakery Oatmeal Raisin
    Cookies, 90
Coconut
Bali Hai Brownies, 21
Carrot Cake Cookies with
    Ginger Cream Cheese Frosting,
    146–147
Chocolate Chip Cookies, 71, *72*, 73
Crazy Cowboy Cookies, 86, *87*
Lamington Bars, 29–30, *31*
Ricotta Coconut Clouds, 46
Coconut Macaroons, 124–125, *125*
Chocolate-Dipped, 126
Chocolate-Drizzled, 125
-Nutella-Almond, *122*, 123
Raspberry, 125
Tribeca Grill's, 126
Coffee
in Brownies, Palm Beach, with
    Chocolate-Covered Mints,
    19–21
in Chocolate Biscotti, Wicked,
    130–131, *131*
and Doughnut Cookies, 183
in Fudge Cookies, Double-
    Chocolate, *106*, 107
Corn Cookies, 150

Cornflake Meringues, Grandma
    Trower's, 115
Crazy Cowboy Cookies, 86, *87*
Cream Cheese
Cheesecake Brownies, *22*, *23*
Frosting, Ginger, 147
Rugelach, Quentin's Grandma's,
    92, 93–95
Whoopie Pies, Red Velvet, *36*,
    37–38
Crescents
of Almond and Cardamom, 57–58
Hungarian, Sugar's, 54, *55*, 56
Kipferl, Almond, *52*, 53
Cutouts, Soft Sugar, 172, *173*

Dairy products, 12–13
DeMasco, Karen, 26, 32, 184
Dorie's Grandmother's Cookies, 171
Double-Chocolate Fudge Chocolate
    Cookies, *106*, 107
Doughnut-Like Cookies
Braids, 180–181
Bugnes de Lyon, 176–177
Cenci, 182
Coffee and Doughnut, 183
Ribbon Cookies, 178–179, *179*

Eggs, and food safety, 14
Eli's Mother's Best Cookies, 162, *163*
English, Todd, 78, 184
Equipment and tools, 10–11
Espresso. *See* Coffee
Everything Cookie, Chocolate
    Chip, 82
Extracts, 12

Fig
Squares, 26, *27*, 28
and Walnut Biscotti, Cinnamon-
    Scented, 128–129
Fitzgerald, Dale Colantropo, 45
Florentine Cookies, *60*, 61
Flour, 12, 13
Flourless Chocolate Cookies,
    104–105, *105*
Fraser, John, 37
French *Macarons*, Raspberry, 118–
    119, *119*
Frosting
Chocolate, 145
Ginger Cream Cheese, 147
Royal Icing, 141
Fruit, Dried

Cherry-Pistachio Oatmeal
    Cookies, *88*, 89
Cherry Surprise Cookies, 77
Fig Bars, 26, *27*
Fig and Walnut Biscotti,
    Cinnamon-Scented, 128–129
Florentine Cookies, *60*, 61
Fudge Cookies, Double-Chocolate,
    106, 107

Gallagher, William, 137
Ganache, Chocolate, 30
Ginger
Bali Hai Brownies, 21
Citrus Cookies, *134*, 135–136
Cream Cheese Frosting, 147
in Molasses Spice Cookies, Sugar-
    Topped, *142*, 143
Gingerbread People, 140–141, *141*
Gingersnap Cookies, 138, *139*
Gingersnaps, 137
Glaze
Chocolate Ganache, 30
Coffee, 183
Honey, 59
Lemon, 46
Orange, 50
Gordon, Isra, 57, 103
Graham Cookies, 149
Grandma Trower's Cornflake
    Meringues, 115
Granny Rennie's Scottish
    Shortbread, 175
Granola Bars, Raspberry, Back-to-
    School, 32–33, *33*
Grausman, Richard, 117, 184
Greenberg, Seth, 167
Greenspan, Dorie, 170, 184
Grunert, Alex, 149, 150, 151
Gutenbrunner, Kurt, 53, 184

Hartnell, Michael, 157
Hazelnuts, in Linzer Cookies, 64–65
Heatter, Maida, 19, 184
Hergatt, Shaun, 29–30, *31*
Humm, Daniel, 89
Hungarian Crescents, Sugar's, 54,
    55, 56

Ice-Cream Sandwiches, 64–65
Icing, Royal, 141
Ingredients
measuring/weighing, 10, 11, 187
pantry staples, 11–12

Ingredients *(cont.)*
  selecting, 12–13
  setup *(mise en place)*, 13–14
  sources for, 187

Jam. *See also* Raspberry Jam
  Bars, 33
  Jammy Dodgers, *156, 157*
  Pistachio Cookies, -Topped, 121
Jammy Dodgers, *156, 157*
Juliet's Kisses, *110*, 111–112

Kaplan, Nicole, 22, 42
Keller, Thomas, 64, 184
Kipferl, Almond, *52, 53*
Kourambiethes, 174

Laiskonis, Michael, 138
Lamington Bars, 29–30, *31*
Lauren's Snickerdoodles, 39
Lemon
  Glaze, 46
  -Poppy Seed Linzers, *152*, 153–154
  Syrup, 180
Levine, Sarabeth, 124, 184
Linzer Cookies, 64–65
  Lemon-Poppy Seed, *152*, 153–154

M&M's, in Monster Cookies, 74, *75*
Macadamia Nut(s)
  Bali Hai Brownies, 21
  Milk Chocolate-Peppermint
    Cookies, 68–69
Macarons
  Pistachio Cookies, 120, *121*
  Pistachio Cookies, Jam-Topped, 121
  Raspberry French, 118–119, *119*
Macaroons. *See* Coconut Macaroons
Maccioni, Egi, 182, 185
Maccioni, Sirio, 182
Madeleines for Alex, 42, *43*
Malgieri, Nick, 17, 185
Malouf, Waldy, 140, 185
Maple Walnut-Pumpkin Cookies, 148
McCarty, Michael, 70, 185
McCoy, Jennifer, 81, 153
Melomakarona, 59
Meringue(s)
  Brutti Ma Buoni, 116
  Cookies, Mint Chocolate Chip,
    Nonny's, 117
  Cornflake, Grandma Trower's, 115
  Pink Swirl and Dusted, *114*, 115
Metric-U.S. conversion chart, 187
Milk Chocolate
  Brownies, *16*, 17–18
  Brownies, Pecan, 18

-Peppermint Macadamia Cookies,
    68–69
Mint. *See* Peppermint
Mise en place, 13–14
Mixers, 10
Molasses
  in Ginger Citrus Cookies, *134*,
    135–136
  in Gingersnap Cookies, 138, *139*
  in Gingersnaps, 137
  in Pumpkin-Maple Walnut
    Cookies, 148
  Spice Cookies, Sugar-Topped,
    142, 143
Monster Cookies, 74, *75*
Moreno, Amanda, 107
Motir, Stéphane, 126
Murphy, Marc, 66

Negrin, Micol, 128, 185
Nicotra, Fortunato, 120
Nonny's Mint Chocolate Chip
  Meringue Cookies, 117
Nut Cookies. *See also* Biscotti
  Crescents of Almond and
    Cardamom, 57–58
  Florentine Cookies, 60, 61
  Hungarian Crescents, Sugar's,
    54, *55*, 56
  Kipferl, Almond, *52*, 53
  Linzer Cookies, 64–65
  Macadamia Milk Chocolate-
    Peppermint Cookies, 68–69
  Melomakarona, 59
  Peanut Butter Cookies, 66, *67*
  Pecan Delights, 70
  Pistachio-Cherry Oatmeal, *88, 89*
  Polvorones, Cashew, 62, *63*
Nutella
  -Almond Coconut Macaroons,
    122, 123
  in Peanut Butter Cookies, 66, *67*
  in Romeo's Sighs and Juliet's
    Kisses, *110*, 111–112

Oatmeal
  Chocolate Chip Everything
    Cookie, 82
  Crazy Cowboy Cookies, 86, *87*
  Granola Bars, Raspberry, Back-to-
    School, 32–33, *33*
  Monster Cookies, 74, *75*
  Pistachio-Cherry Cookies, *88, 89*
  Raisin Cookies, City Bakery, 90
Olson, Nancy, 74
Ong, Pichet, 71, 123, 185
Orange Cookies, 48, 49–50

Palm Beach Brownies with
  Chocolate-Covered Mints,
  19–21
Palmiers, 96–97
Pastry
  Puff, for Palmiers, 96–97
  Rugelach, Quentin's Grandma's,
    92, 93–95
Payard, François, 47, 104, 185
Peach Compote, *Trao-Mad* with,
  158–159
Peanut Butter
  Cookies, 66, *67*
  Monster Cookies, 74, *75*
Pecan(s)
  Brownies, Milk Chocolate, 18
  in Carrot Cake Cookies with
    Ginger Cream Cheese Frosting,
    146–147
  in Chocolate Chip Everything
    Cookie, 82
  and Chocolate Cookies, 108, *109*
  in Chocolate Knobs, 103
  in Chumleys, *24, 25*
  Delights, 70
  in Granola Bars, Raspberry, Back-
    to-School, 32–33, *33*
Peel, Candied. *See* Citrus Peel,
  Candied
Peppermint
  Chocolate-Covered Mints, Palm
    Beach Brownies with, 19–21
  -Milk Chocolate Macadamia
    Cookies, 68–69
  Mint Chocolate Chip Meringue
    Cookies, Nonny's, 117
Petits Fours
  à l'Anise, 100
  de Noël, 101–102
  Tea Cakes Pineapple, 47
Pineapple Tea Cakes, 47
Pinkerton, Angela, 54
Pink Swirl and Dusted Meringues,
  114, 115
Piping bags, 10–11
Pistachio(s)
  -Cherry Oatmeal Cookies, *88, 89*
  in Chocolate Biscotti, Wicked,
    130–131, *131*
  Cookies, 120, *121*
  Cookies, Jam-Topped, 121
  in Fudge Cookies, Double-
    Chocolate, *106*, 107
Pizzelle, *164*, 165–166
Pizzettes, 144–145
Poilâne, Lionel, 170
Polvorones, Cashew, 62, *63*

Poppy Seed-Lemon Linzers, *152,*
153–154
Puff Pastry, for Palmiers, 96–97
Pumpkin-Maple Walnut Cookies,
148
Pumpkin Seed and Red Fife
Cookies, 151
Punitions, 170–171

Quentin's Grandma's Rugelach, *92,*
93–95

Raisin(s)
in Carrot Cake Cookies with
Ginger Cream Cheese Frosting,
146–147
Oatmeal Cookies, City Bakery, 90
Rugelach, Quentin's Grandma's,
92, 93–94
Raspberry Coconut Macaroons, 125
Raspberry Jam
Chocolate Filling, Rugelach,
Quentin's Grandma's, *92,* 94–95
Granola Bars, Back-to-School,
32–33, *33*
in Lamington Bars, 29–30, *31*
Macarons, French, 118–119, *119*
in Romeo's Sighs and Juliet's
Kisses, *110,* 111–112
in Thumbprint Cookies, Classic,
The Baker Man's, 167–168, *169*
Red Fife and Pumpkin Seed
Cookies, 151
Red Velvet Whoopie Pies, *36,* 37–38
Ribbon Cookies, 178–179, *179*
Ricotta
Chip Cookies, 46
Coconut Clouds, 46
Cookies, *44,* 45–46
Sammies, 46
Rizzo, Grace, 144, 180
Rodriguez, Kir, 62
Romeo's Sighs and Juliet's Kisses,
110, 111–112
Royal Icing, 141
Rubin, Maury, 90, 185
Rugelach, Quentin's Grandma's, *92,*
93–95

Sailhac, Alain, 96
Samuelsson, Marcus, 135, 185
Sandwich Cookies
Chocolate Chip Banana, *80,* 81
Ice-Cream, 64–65
Jammy Dodgers, *156,* 157
Lemon-Poppy Seed Linzers, *152,*
153–154

Macadamia Milk Chocolate-
Peppermint, 68–69
Macarons, Raspberry French,
118–119, *119*
Peanut Butter, 66, *67*
Ricotta Sammies, 46
Romeo's Sighs and Juliet's Kisses,
110, 111–112
Whoopie Pies, 34–35
Whoopie Pies, Red Velvet, *36,*
37–38
Sandys, 76
Santana, Amar, 146
Scale, 11
Scoops, 10
Scottish Shortbread, Granny
Rennie's, 175
Seed Cookies
Poppy Seed-Lemon Linzers, *152,*
153–154
Pumpkin Seed and Red Fife, 151
Sheet pans, 10
Shelbo, Jen, 172
Shortbread
Jammy Dodgers, *156,* 157
Kourambiethes, 174
Poppy Seed, 153
Scottish, Granny Rennie's, 175
Smith, Risa, 93
Snickerdoodles, *40,* 41
Lauren's, 39
Soft Sugar Cutouts, 172, *173*
Soltner, André, 100, 185
Spice Cookies
Carrot Cake, with Ginger Cream
Cheese Frosting, 146–147
Gingerbread People, 140–141, *141*
Ginger Citrus, *134,* 135–136
Gingersnap Cookies, 138, *139*
Gingersnaps, 137
Graham, 149
Molasses, Sugar-Topped, *142,* 143
Pizzettes, 144–145
Pumpkin-Maple Walnut, 148
Squares. *See* Bars and Squares
Stupak, Alex, 39
Sugar, 12
Cinnamon, 178
-Topped Molasses Spice Cookies,
142, 143
Sugar Cookies
Cutouts, Soft Sugar, 172, *173*
Dorie's Grandmother's, 171
Eli's Mother's Best Cookies, 162,
163
Jammy Dodgers, *156,* 157
Pizzelle, *164,* 165–166

Punitions, 170–171
Thumbprint, Classic, The Baker
Man's, 167–168, *169*
Trao-Mad with Peach Compote,
158–159
Valentines, Sugar, *160,* 161
Sugar's Hungarian Crescents, 54,
55, 56
Syrup, 59, 180

Tampakis, Michelle, 59, 174
Tasker, Mark, 175
Tea Cakes, Pineapple, 47
Tempered chocolate, 12
Thornton, Jerry, 178
Thumbprint Cookies, Classic, The
Baker Man's, 167–168, *169*
Todd's Favorite Triple Chocolate
and Walnut Cookies, 78, *79*
Torres, Jacques, 83, 185
Tourondel, Laurent, 143, 185
Trao-Mad with Peach Compote,
158–159
Tribeca Grill's Coconut Macaroons,
126
Truitt, Robert, 82

Valentines, Sugar, *160,* 161
Valenti, Tom, 41, 185
Vongerichten, Jean-Georges, 98, 185

Walnut(s)
Biscotti, and Fig, Cinnamon-
Scented, 128–129
Brownies, Palm Beach, with
Chocolate-Covered Mints,
19–21
and Chocolate Cookies, Triple,
Todd's Favorite, 78, *79*
Chocolate Cookies, Flourless,
104–105, *105*
Maple, -Pumpkin Cookies, 148
Melomakarona, 59
Rugelach, Quentin's Grandma's,
92, 93–95
Waxman, Jonathan, 68, 185
Weiner, Jason, 93
Whoopie Pies, 34–35
Red Velvet, *36,* 37–38
Wicked Chocolate Biscotti, 130–131,
131

Zabar, David, 77
Zabar, Eli, 162
Zabar, Tracey, 25, 34, 76, 111, 115,
130, 161, 165

First published in the United States
of America in 2011 by Rizzoli
International Publications, Inc.
300 Park Avenue South
New York, New York 10010
www.rizzoliusa.com

2011 2012 2013 2014 /
10 9 8 7 6 5 4 3 2 1

Printed in China

ISBN 13: 978-0-8478-3666-6

Library of Congress Control Number:
2011927545

Project Editor: Sandra Gilbert
Graphic design by Jan Derevjanik

CREDITS

The following publishers and authors
have kindly granted permission (with
all rights reserved) for Tracey Zabar to
include adaptations of their previously
published recipes in One Sweet Cookie.

PAGE 19 PALM BEACH BROWNIES WITH
CHOCOLATE-COVERED MINTS
Maida Heatter's Brand-New Book of Great
Cookies. Random House, Inc. ©1995
Maida Heatter. Used by permission
of the author.

PAGE 32 BACK-TO-SCHOOL RASPBERRY
GRANOLA BARS
The Craft of Baking: Cakes, Cookies and
Other Sweets with Ideas for Inventing Your
Own. ©2009 Karen DeMasco and
Mindy Fox. Used by permission of
Clarkson Potter/Publishers, an imprint
of the Crown Publishing Group,
a division of Random House, Inc.

PAGE 41 SNICKERDOODLES
You Don't Have to be Diabetic to Love this
Cookbook. ©2009 Tom Valenti and
Andrew Friedman. Used by permission
of Workman Publishing Company, Inc.

PAGE 47 PINEAPPLE TEA CAKES
Simply Sensational Desserts: 140 Classics for
the Home Baker from New York's Famous
Patisserie and Bistro. ©1999 François
Payard. Clarkson Potter/Publishers.
Used by permission of the author.

PAGE 64 ICE-CREAM SANDWICHES
Ad Hoc at Home. ©2009 Thomas Keller.
Used by permission of Artisan,
a division of Workman Publishing
Company, Inc.

PAGE 70 PECAN DELIGHTS
Michael's Cookbook: The Art of New
American Food and Entertaining. ©1989
Michael McCarty. Used by permission
of John Wiley & Sons, Inc.

PAGE 71 COCONUT CHOCOLATE CHIP
COOKIES
The Sweet Spot: Asian-Inspired Desserts.
©2007 Pichet Ong and Genevieve
Ko. Used by permission of William
Morrow, an imprint of HarperCollins
Publishers.

PAGE 83 CHOCOLATE CHIP COOKIES
Jacques Torres' A Year in Chocolate: 80
Recipes for Holidays and Special Occasions.
©2008 Jacques Torres and Judith
Choate. Used by permission of Stewart,
Tabori & Chang, an imprint of Harry
N. Abrams, Inc.

PAGES 100–01 PETITS FOURS À L'ANISE
AND PETITS FOURS DE NOËL
The Lutèce Cookbook. ©1995 André
Soltner and Seymour Britchky. Used
by permission of Alfred A. Knopf,
a division of Random House, Inc.

PAGE 104 FLOURLESS CHOCOLATE COOKIES
Chocolate Epiphany: Exceptional Cookies,
Cakes, and Confections for Everyone.
©2008 François Payard with Anne
E. McBride. Used by permission of
Clarkson Potter/Publishers, an imprint
of the Crown Publishing Group,
a division of Random House, Inc.

PAGE 116 BRUTTI MA BUONI
True Tuscan: Flavors and Memories from
the Countryside of Tuscany. ©2005
Cesare Casella. Used by permission
of HarperCollins Publishers.

PAGE 132 BISCOTTI ALLE MANDORLE
My Love for Naples. ©2007 Anna
Teresa Callen. Used by permission
of Hippocrene Books, Inc.

PAGE 135 GINGER CITRUS COOKIES
Acquavit and the New Scandinavian
Cuisine. By Marcus Samuelsson. ©2003
Townhouse Restaurant Group. Used
by permission of Houghton Mifflin
Harcourt Publishing Company.

PAGES 158 AND 176 TRAO-MAD WITH PEACH
COMPOTE AND BUGNES DE LYON
Daniel Boulud's Café Boulud Cookbook:
French-American Recipes for the Home
Cook. ©1999 Daniel Boulud and
Dorie Greenspan. Used by permission
of Scribner, a division of Simon &
Schuster, Inc.

PAGE 162 ELI'S MOTHER'S BEST COOKIES
The Barefoot Contessa Cookbook. ©1999
Ina Garten. Used by permission of
Clarkson Potter/Publishers, an imprint
of the Crown Publishing Group,
a division of Random House, Inc.

PAGE 170 PUNITIONS
Paris Sweets: Great Desserts from the
City's Best Pastry Shops. ©2002 Dorie
Greenspan. Used by permission of
Broadway Books, a division of Random
House, Inc.

PAGE 182 CENCI
The Maccioni Family Cookbook: Recipes
and Memories from an Italian-American
Kitchen. ©2003 Egi Maccioni with
Peter Kaminsky. Used by permission of
Stewart, Tabori & Chang, an imprint
of Harry N. Abrams, Inc.